M000205601

HIDDEN
秘伝

A SERIES OF SCIENTIFIC ARTICLES ON SECRET TECHNIQUES AND TACTICS OF
JAPANESE – OKINAWAN MARTIAL ARTS

Author: Mosi Dorbayani, PhD - Soke

著者: モシ.ドルバヤニ, 宗家

Publisher: The Academy of Scientific Martial Arts

Canada & Hungary – European Union

版元: 科学的な武術スキルのアカデミー

Library and Archives Canada

ISBN: 978-0-9940842-0-0

http://renmei.wix.com/kojido
www.facebook.com/kojidorenmei

Brushed on canvas by the author: Sun, Moon & the Path

This book is dedicated to you.

TABLE OF CONTENTS

FOREWORD

BY TETSUHIRO HOKAMA, PhD, Hanshi, 10th Dan

President of Okinawa International Kobudo Organisation – IKO
Okinawa International Goju-Ryu Kenshi-Kai
Founder of World's First Karate Museum and Reference Hall

The longer martial artists keep practicing, the more imperative the martial arts' literature becomes for them.

For a beginner, at first everything may seem physical exercise without knowing or being told why, but as they pave their chosen martial path and progress, curiosity increases and questions start to rise. They will naturally look for meanings and they want to know more about the essence and reasons on what they do.

I am 70 years old now but I clearly recall my youth, when I was not convinced with the Bunkai (application of Kata) as I was first being taught and kept questioning the applications.

I was blessed by learning from grandmasters such as 'Seiko Higa', a student of 'Kanryo Higaonna' (1853-1915) and 'Chojun Miyagi' (1888-1953) as well as 'Shinpo Matayoshi', (1922-1997). It was both of those great masters who recognized my eagerness and taught me the '*Kakushite* 隠し手' (hidden hand) the secret techniques in Kata.

I was 35 when I opened my dojo in Okinawa and thus far I have conducted Kobudo and Karate seminars in 42 countries. However I wrote and co-published 76 books on martial arts, I had never written a scientific one. But Dr. Mosi Dorbayani, Soke – really fascinated me with his excellent analysis in this publication. From definitions to history, from human biomechanics to strategies. This is what I call a truly unprecedented "Scientific writing" for martial arts. Every article in this book is a reply to many unanswered questions that one might have; therefore, I hope every martial artist studies it in depth.

By Chris Glenn,

Lecturer, Author and Samurai Historian based in Nagoya, Japan
A member of the Japan Armor and Weapons Research and Preservation Society
Yudansha in Kendo and Practitioner of Enmei Ryu and *Owari Yagyu Shinkage Ryu*

"Foreigners learn the martial arts thinking that it is good to fight. That is not right." This was a comment made by my Sensei during an interview I translated some years back.

The martial arts of Japan are revered, indeed the word "samurai" is instantly recognizable across the world. The samurai are seen as exceptionally brave and dedicated, highly skilled fighters with superb weaponry and armor. Men of the sword, and the pen, in accord. Practitioners of the martial arts, but men of culture, just as dedicated to literature, the visual and performing arts, and the delicate tea ceremony as they are their weapons. They could indeed be seen as true heroes, the ideal human being, someone to truly admire and look up to.

The Japanese Koryu, traditional martial arts, are among the world's most refined and practiced fighting systems. Although established in times of war, many of the Koryu systems advocated not the killing of another, but merely stopping the opposition.

Indeed, as I have written in my book, 豪州人歴史愛好家、名城を行く (pub: Takarashima-Sha, Tokyo, 2015) the greatest defense of a Japanese castle is not it's magnificent keep, nor its many watchtowers, impressive gates and sturdy stone walls, but its reputation.

A castle's reputation as a strong, well-designed and defended establishment would have prevented an enemy from even considering attacking. So too are the martial arts, a way to achieve peace through learning to fight, in the hope that these skills will not need to be used.

Dedicated study of the samurai, their history and culture, and the true meaning of their martial systems, and scientific studies of martial strategies destroys a lot of the popular culture romance and mystique.

The samurai were brave, loyal and dedicated. But they were not infallible, nor were they without foibles. I hope that readers of this book will remember that the samurai, just like you and I, were after all, human.

This calligraphy is brushed by Grandmaster Tetsuhiro Hokama, a congratulatory token for this book.
It means 'Science of Martial Arts' – the subtitle of this publication

PREFACE

Usually when the term *'Martial Arts'* is mentioned, inevitably the fighting arts of Eastern Asia comes to mind. This is perhaps due to popular culture and influences of movies and media. In fact, the term 'martial arts', comes from the Latin 'Mars / Martis', meaning 'God of War', which is an ancient Roman religion and myth.[1] It refers to the European combat system which dates back to 1500s.

A statue of Mars with his 'Spear and Shield'

Historically, the roots of 'martial arts,' predominantly goes far back to the ancient Greece, Egypt, Persia and India. The ancient artifacts and recorded history indicate that the martial arts and the art of weaponry have existed in those countries for thousands of years.

Egyptian Mural for a tomb at Beni Hasan, Dated around 2000 BC - Showing wrestlers

6

India, Uttar Pradesh, 5th century Sculpture – Combat-wrestling

The oldest artifact that depicts scenes of battle is the ancient Egyptian paintings showing some sort of struggle dated 3400 BC.[2] A similar artifact in Mesopotamia (Babylon) is dated 3000 BC.[3] Elsewhere, in Vietnam, sketches from 2879 BC, show certain ways of combat with the use of a sword, staff, bows and spears.[4] Among ancient practices that are still being exercised today, we can name *'Kushti Pahlevani'* (Warriors' wrestling) of Persia and India, which has its roots in *'Malla-Yuddah'* (Combat wrestling) dated back to the 5th millennium BC.[5]

Yellow Emperor, Huang Di

Chinese martial arts originated during the Xia Dynasty. It is said that the Yellow Emperor, 'Huang Di' (Reign 2698–2598 BC) introduced the earliest fighting systems to China. Huang Di is described as a famous intellectual and a wise general who had written many materials on medicine, astrology and the combative arts[6] before becoming China's Emperor.

Sun Tzu in 'The Art of War' (c. 350 BC)[7] describes that an extensive development in 'martial philosophy' and 'martial strategy' emerged during the period of Chinese 'Warring States' (480-221 BC). Evidently, the foundation of modern Asian martial arts is a blend of early Chinese and Indian martial arts. Some accounts link the origin of '***Shaolin Quan*** 少林拳'the oldest institutionalized form of '***Wushu*** 武術' (Chinese Martial Arts) to the spread of Buddhism from India to China during the early 5th century AD.[8]

Shitsukongo-shin, Painted Clay Nara Period

The preserved artifacts, records and documents [9] in Japan indicate that *'Gungaku Heiho* 軍学兵法*'* (Military / Martial Strategies) have existed at least since 8th century, the Nara Era (710 – 794), and such martial strategies, 'Daibun or Shobun' (Group or Individual strategy) got heavily influenced by 'Buddhism' from China, which officially became a permanent religion in Japan during the same period, as well as the native 'Shinto' and various studies of 'Taoism' and 'Yin & Yang' (*In-yo* 陰陽 in Japanese).

During the Meiji Era (1868 – 1912) Japanese nation quickly changed from a feudal to a modernized industrial state of democracy; hence, the dynamics of Warrior's class ruling Japan abolished and especially after World War II (1939 – 1945), the teaching of traditional martial strategies declined.

In a number of classical martial art schools in Japan and a few in the West, the ancient techniques and tactics have been successfully transmitted to this very day and they are well preserved, but this is often not the case for many training centers, especially outside Japan.

Although the number of martial arts enthusiasts around the world has increased, and in many countries they are often being taught by qualified instructors, sadly many technical, tactical and above all, the core spirit of genuine martial arts are omitted from the Japanese and Okinawan martial strategies.

This was simply to suit the art for the mass practice, i.e. to turn the martial arts into a form of physical fitness and education at schools and to a Western competitive martial sport or game, based on winning rather than surviving or self-defense.

Head and arm lock in Ishiguro Ryu Jujutsu

However the transition from '***Bujutsu*** 武術' (Martial Arts/Skills) to '***Budo*** 武道' (Martial Way) and martial sport both in Japan and the West spiced with Hollywood movies caused a huge popularity in general, it regretfully brought a decline in the true teaching of '***Koryu Bujutsu*** 古流武術' (Old school or Traditional Martial Arts) and to some degree faded the historical, spiritual, educational and scientific values of various martial traditions.

Samurai practicing Bo/Sojutsu (Staff / Spear) - 1700s

Of course it is simply true that many aspects of martial strategies both in mainland Japan and in Okinawa (Ryukyu) were kept secret for centuries and it was not until late 19th and the early 20th century, when they opened up their doors to the public or outsiders and shared their martial traditions, but still after so many years and thousands of publications or media productions, we can see that many scientific, tactical, and spiritual aspects of Japanese martial strategies are widely misunderstood and surprisingly at times misinterpreted or misrepresented even inside Japan.

As mentioned earlier, fortunately there are several centers and martial schools that are still carrying the traditions by teaching the genuine spirit behind the creation of techniques, and preserving their strategies in their curriculums in a way that eventually, *'the art of war, becomes the art of peace'*.

Nawajutsu - Japanese martial art of restraining a person using cord or rope

Such traditional centers and their approach to martial strategies inspired me to share my studies, views and experience to facilitate a better understanding of 'Bujutsu'.

Therefore, in this publication I will focus on Japanese-Okinawan martial arts and strategies, which in my opinion are not only delicate and sophisticated, but also classically stand the test of time.

Employing the modern science and theories, in this book I will try to address and explain a few basics, yet fundamental aspects of traditional martial technique and tactics, which are often misunderstood or simply overlooked.

While this literature consists of various independent articles and they each can be studied separately, readers are encouraged to begin with paper 1. The 'conclusion' for each paper is kept short, so that readers can contemplate more and perhaps draw their own conclusion.

However this descriptive publication can be suitable for all adults with interest in traditional martial arts, it may be found particularly useful by those with martial arts experience and interest in the academic aspects of martial strategies.

Hereby, I would like to thank all who made this publication possible and those who supported me with their words of encouragement and endorsements. My appreciation to 'Tetsuhiro Hokama, Hanshi' and 'Chris Glenn, Yudansha' for their contributions in this publication.

I wish to express my gratitude to those, who inspired me to study Koryu:

- **Kuroda Tetsuzan, Soke** – Shinbukan Kuroda Dojo
- **Kyoso Shigetoshi, Shihan** - Tenshinsho-den Katori Shinto-ryu

I would like to extend my appreciation to the followings for the demonstration of their stellar arts, their shared written and oral traditions, publications and teachings, which influenced and impressed me.

From Tenshinsho-den Katori Shinto-ryu Headquarters:

- Iizasa Yasusada, Soke;
- Risuke Otake, Shihan;
- Nobutoshi Otake, Shihan;

From Yagyu Shingan-ryu Heihojutsu Kyodensho Chikuosha:

- Shimazu Kenji, Soke

From Daito-ryu Aiki Jujutsu:

- Katsuyuki Kondo, Kyoju Dairi

Furthermore, my respect goes to:

Late Dr. Farhad Varaste, Soke of Kanzen-ryu; Late Kenji Kusano, Soke of Kusano Ha Shito-ryu Kenpo; Late Manzo Iwata, President of Shitokai. Also I would like to extend my courtesy to Lee Sensei, Greg Wallace Shihan; my youth martial sport coaches: H. Ebrahimi & G. Kamangir; my uncles Reza and Abbas Dorbayani, who encouraged me to take up martial arts at very young age. Also my praise goes to British All Styles Karate Association, Hungarian Karate Federation, European Sogo Budo Federation, Tatami Centrum, Intl Ryukyu Karate Research Society, Okinawa Karate Museum, The Hawaii Karate Museum, and Okinawa Intl. Hokama Kobudo Organization.

PAPER 1

KIAI: A CRY FOR UNITY

Visiting almost any Martial Arts training dojo or event, one would inevitably hear that practitioners often yell during their 'Kumite' (Fight) while practicing their 'Randori' (Drills) or at some points, when performing 'Kata' (Forms). This is commonly known as '**Kiai** 気合' (Ya Gi in Okinawan).

Kyoso Shigetoshi, Shihan - Katori Shinto-Ryu
Public Demo at Meiji Jingu –
Delivering an Iai cut with Kiai

Less experienced teachers of Martial Arts, especially in the West, often describe 'Kiai' as a shout from the throat to distract the opponent, or a sound similar to the effort of lifting a heavy object. And they often reason by saying because some techniques are heavy and powerful, hence the need for such yell/sound to complement their execution.

Well, the fact of the matter is that 'Kiai' is well beyond such descriptions and it can be studied and defined, 'Linguistically', 'Technically', 'Philosophically', 'Scientifically' or even 'Historically', both inside and outside the domain of martial arts.

THE DEFINITION:

Before everything, while it is alright to use 'Shout' or 'Yell' to address Kiai, I would rather use the word 'Cry' hereafter, simply because it is closer to the reality of its functionality. In the English language, Oxford dictionary defines the word 'Cry', among others, as:

- *a loud <u>inarticulate</u> shout or scream expressing a <u>powerful feeling or emotion</u>*
- *a <u>demand or opinion</u> expressed by <u>many people</u>*

Having the above two definitions in mind, now let us explore the word Kiai in the Japanese language. According to Jisho dictionary:

- *'**Ki** 気' (in Chinese Qi / Chi) is literally translated as: Air, Aura, Spirit or Energy*
- *'**Ai** 合' is literally translated as: Combine, Unite, or Join*

Putting the two together, it can be said that Kiai is the act of *'unifying energy'*.

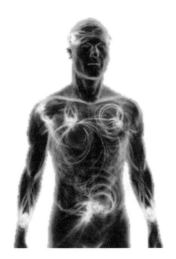

But certainly this unifying energy doesn't make much sense, especially for a Non-Martial Artist reader; unless, it is either applied before them or explained deeper, right? So, what is the application or action for Kiai? Well, now that we are clear about the word itself, let us first take a few steps back to analyze *a couple of equally crucial inter-related subjects* before attending the application and action of Kiai and its vocalization.

KI – ELEMENTS:

In traditional Chinese culture, Qi (Chi) (Ki in Japanese) is the *'Natural Energy'* or *'Life Force'*. In the West, it is also called *'The Force'* as often used in Hollywood movies such as Star Wars or *'Vitalism'* / *'Energeia'* or simply *'Energy'* in the same notion.

'It is the flow of energy that sustains living beings'.

From the *'philosophical'* point of view, this concept can be traced back to the records of Chinese Philosophy in

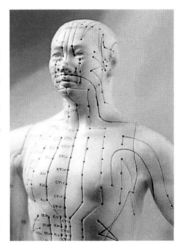

Ki / Chi Pathways

the 5th Century BC and the ancient Hindo Yogic concept of Prana (Life Force) in Sanskrit. An early form of the idea comes from the writings of the Chinese philosopher Mencius (4th century BC).

'Historically', also the Huangdi Neijing / *"The Yellow Emperor's Classic of Medicine"* (circa 2nd century BC) is credited with first establishing the pathways through which Qi/Ki circulates in the human body.[10]

So, where the ancient Chinese describes it as "life force", the common belief is that Qi/Ki allows everything to get linked to their surroundings together. This linkage in the flow of energy around and through the body is forming a cohesive and functioning unit. Hence, by understanding its **'rhythm'** and **'flow'** one can guide exercises and treatments to provide stability and longevity.

On another note, in the *'Analects of Confucius'*: the collection of sayings and ideas attributed to the Chinese philosopher, *Confucius* and his contemporaries, which is believed to have been written by Confucius' followers (475 BC–221 BC), there is a text reading: Qi could mean **"breath"**, and it came combined with the Chinese word for blood (making 血氣, xue-qi, blood and breath).[11]

So, with view to the above, here we have three important elements to consider:

1. **Flow of energy;**

2. **Rhythm of energy;**

3. **Breathing.**

- What is flow of energy? *Flow of energy is actually transferring cells with 'Higher energy' in content to cells with 'Lower energy' in content.*

- What is rhythm of energy? *Rhythm of energy is the sequence and frequency of transferring 'high energy cells' to the 'low energy cells' in content.*

- And what is the breathing role here? *Well, breathing is the most crucial part of developing Qi/Ki energy. When one breathes in, the blood pressure goes up and when breathes out, the blood pressure goes down. The interval action of breathing lets the air flow in the body and energizes it.*

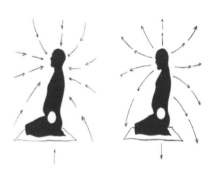

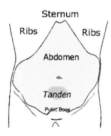

Breathing with a proper flow and rhythm will also create heat, a warm feeling or energy. And by using our 'Mind' in a concentrated manner, we can direct that energy to a targeted area, which can be found healing. Qi/Ki is located in the center of our body called **'Tanden'** ('Dantian' in Chinese and 'Hara' in Japanese). It is located in the lower belly, a few inches lower than the navel, in the middle, inside. It is the so-called 'Battery' of our body. It requires charging and maintenance; therefore, concentration / meditation and breathing exercises are required especially for the Martial Artists to develop their Qi/Ki energy.

Speaking of concentration and meditation, do **'Brain and Mind'** have any deeper role in this? Absolutely. As we know, the Earth has a frequency of **7.83 Hertz**. *The human brain also has the same frequency of 7.83 Hertz!* This is known as *'Schumann Resonance'* - the success of therapy with 7.83 Hertz pulsating magnetic fields very clearly demonstrates the importance of this frequency.

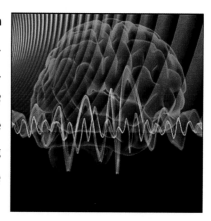

The human brain in a healthy state has also been shown to oscillate at 7.83 Hertz. Consequently, our brains are in a natural state of resonance with the earth. The loss of this characteristic would result in significant limitations to our vitality and health.[12]

Once you connect and harmonize your energy and frequency with the frequency of the nature, you get empowered for physical activities.

That is why we often feel good, when we are out in the nature, because our frequency gets connected to the frequency of the earth and we get empowered.

KOKYU - BREATHING:

In the study of Kiai, the first and foremost critical subject to note is the '***Kokyu*** 呼吸' (Breathing) System.

Here we can name four levels of breathing:

1. **Lung Breathing:** It is what we do normally and unconsciously. It is noted by expansion of air in the chest area.

2. **Lower Abdomen Breathing:** It is directed towards breathing into the lower abdomen by letting the diaphragm to lower, when expanding the lungs, giving the abdominal expansion.

3. **Tension Breathing:** It is breathing into abdominal contraction with tension being used on exhalation.

4. **Passive Breathing:** also known as "Dead Breathing" is breathing without using the diaphragm. This level is very difficult to accomplish, yet important to learn especially for battlefields and camouflage situations.

In Martial Arts, especially those such as Karate, the breathing principles are divided into two categories:

Nogare: it is a normal breathing, inhaling and exhaling through the nose. It has a quiet and natural sound and it utilizes tension with relaxation in the muscles, which provides the power needed for strong and rapid execution of techniques as well as quick body movement. This type of breathing is usually seen in Okinawa Shuri-styles of Karate.

*Arcenio J. Advincula Performing
Sanchin Kata, 1979*

- **Ibuki:** it is breathing in the nose but exhaling through the mouth. It is loud and slightly hissing in sound. It also utilizes tension with relaxation in the muscles, and gives the practitioner natural yet defined and exaggerated movements. This type of breathing is usually seen in Okinawa Naha-styles of Karate.

Certainly 'Nogare' and 'Ibuki' are not limited to Karate and can be noticed in Wushu, Kenpo as well as Taekwondo. The above two categories have roots in the Chinese Martial Arts especially in various styles of 'White Crane' and even certain traditional Tai-Chi.

With view to all the above, since the '*Ki* 気' (first syllabus/first part) of 'Kiai' is directing us to 'Air' and 'Energy'; therefore, now it would be easier to realize that the breathing system plays an important role in the concept of 'Kiai'.

As mentioned earlier, there are a few crucial points to know before attending the application of Kiai. Now that we put the 'Definitions', the 'Concept of Ki' and the 'Breathing Systems' out of the way, we can talk about the second most important element here. And that is '**Kime**'.

KIME - NEUROMUSCULAR CONTRACTION:

'**Kime** 決め' comes from the Japanese word '**Kimeru** 決める' meaning 'To Decide'. While in the East it is often known as 'Extreme Decision' or 'Maximum Focus Energy', in the West, the Science of Biomechanics defines it as *'Short Isometric Neuromuscular Contraction'*.[13]

To perform a technique with good 'Kime', one requires to quickly tense the muscles, i.e. to snap them at the moment of impact, but not too hard to cause muscles to shake.

The ability to co-ordinate muscles to snap and relax before and after the technique, translates itself into 'Kime'. So, with this and the definition above in mind, now we are getting much closer to the application and action of Kiai.

Have you seen a Martial Artist doing a 'Kata' (form) and their 'Gi' (uniform) snaps or makes a whoosh sound?

Well, if not using cinematic sound effect or cheating, the main reason for hearing snap/whoosh sounds is that: the Muscular Contraction for that particular action is 'narrow', 'short' and 'high in speed', hence the sound of snap/whoosh.

This may as well be felt and heard in Kenjutsu and Iaido forms, when the Katana makes the whoosh sound cutting the air.[14]

Such demonstration of power shows the intense level of 'Kime', and the timely well-executed Isometric Neuromuscular Contraction makes a technique very powerful.

Tameshigiri / Suemono Giri

Shiwari (breaking hard objects) in Karate

A good Kime also can be sensed or felt during '*Shiwari*' (breaking hard objects) or '*Tameshigiri / Suemono Giri*' (Cutting fixed objects / Cutting Test). None of which can be properly done without 'Kime'.

Now, what is the connection between 'Kime' and 'Kokyu' (Breathing)?

Well, for human beings in order to move, they need 'Muscles' and 'Energy'. As described in the concept of 'Ki', we get the vital energy from the 'Air'. There are over **'640 Muscles'** in the human body, and most of them are involved in breathing.

For Martial Artists, generating and utilizing energy and on top of that transferring the right amount of it through the muscles to the opponent are quite crucial. They require a skillful co-ordination of concentration, breathing, muscles contraction and proper speed and timing.

THE ACTION AND SOUNDS OF KIAI:

Now that we briefly addressed 'Ki', 'Kokyu', and 'Kime' and learnt a few things about them, it is easier to describe and understand the act of 'Kiai'.

Well, the action is exactly as the definition suggests: "unifying our viable energy". BUT unifying energy to or with what?

Kiai is the act of unifying 'Ki=Energy' (mostly gained through breathing air) with 'Physical movements / Technique (often performed by Muscles)'.

So, now you can see that it's not simply a "shout from the throat" as some teachers may put it.

For those who practice Aiki (Aiki Jutsu / Aikido) it is important to remember that there is an absolute equality between Kiai & Aiki. During an impact, you feel Kiai but Aiki is what your opponent feels. This is also known as '***Kiroku*** 気力'(Power of Ki / Willpower). It is when the Ki energy is felt by one person from another at the time of impact during the execution of a technique. Those who are advanced in applying Ki, have '***Kihaku*** [Tamashi] 気魂 (Spirit of Ki) and they can draw the Ki of their opponent to overcome them.

Now, having said all that, why the Cry sound? Well, the fact of the matter is 'unifying our viable energy, i.e. Kiai' could be silent or loud! But here, I first explain the form of Kiai with sound - (Vocalized Kiai):

Do you remember the first underlining definition of 'cry' in the English language at the beginning of this paper? Yes, "*a loud <u>inarticulate</u> shout expressing a powerful feeling or emotion.*"

Often when Martial Artists are on their maximum focus, transferring their energy (Ki) through their body and delivering an attack, a counter attack or a block with 'Kime', their powerful high spirited action at the time of exhaling and body contraction comes with a loud <u>inarticulate</u> sound. Often sounds like: 'Iyaaa', 'Ieeee'; 'Yeeee'; 'Heyyyy'; 'Taaaa'; etc. **But why such sounds?!**

SOUNDS IN KIAI:

First the reason behind the sound:

The records of Music proves: Music is produced by sound, the root of which is in human being's mind, feelings, and senses towards their environment, things and surroundings. Hence, when human beings feel happiness, their voices are cheerful; when they feel sad or in sorrow their voices are choked; when in anger, their voices are harsh; and <u>when excited, their voices are expansive.</u>

To 'Cry' in or for a situation, is not new to human being. As long as we remember, we know that people often 'cry for help', 'shout to give notice/warning', and 'make a sound or a noise to express themselves'.

Outside the Martial Arts domain for example, people might cry for help when they are in danger. They might shout to give a warning to a friend before falling into a trap or make noises by banging objects to cause distraction or even give signals etc.

So, screaming, shouting, crying, making noises can all be interpreted as a type of <u>'Defense Mechanism'</u> for human being. But why the vocalization of Kiai in Martial Arts?

In the context of Martial Arts, a vocalized Kiai is to some extent more than a human defense mechanism.

It is among others, a sort of strategy and technique which can be:

- **Interruptive**
- **Destructive**
- **Communicative**

Is there any science behind it? Of course there is. Nothing is without reason. As a person in love with Martial Science and Martial Strategy, I did some research and found very interesting reasons behind the vocalized Kiai.

Katori Shrine

My interest and studies in Koryu (Old School / Traditional Martial Arts) led me to one of the oldest styles in Japan, *'Tenshinsho-den Katori Shinto-ryu'*- a 600-year-old Bujutsu School.[15] The very first thing I noticed in Katori Shinto-ryu was how their vocalized Kiai is different from what I had experienced in other Martial Ways or even Martial Sports.

In Katori Shinto-ryu and its descendant arts such as Kashinma Shinto-ryu or Shinto Muso-ryu, they often use sounds like: **'Ei'**; **'Ya'**, **'Tou'** and sometimes: **'Ei - Hot/Hod'** or **'Eiya – Hod'**. This is also similar for other Koryu styles such as Yagyu Shingan-ryu and Daito-ryu Aiki Jujutsu schools that I studied.[16]

Luckily during the research on this subject, the experience from my hobby came in handy. As a Lyricist, I learnt about the importance of sounds, especially the Vowels (A.E.I.O.U) in writing lyrics for Tenors and Sopranos.

I often need to pay careful attention when putting words together for a verse and I need to make sure words have best possible vowels for the singer or the recording artist to get the chance to use the sound of vowels for better and clearer <u>vibrato</u>.

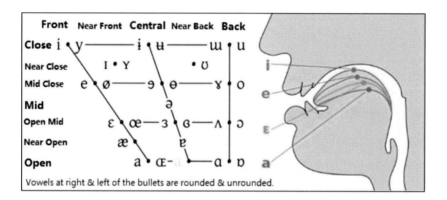

The sound **'Ei'** is often vocalized at the start or initiation of a martial technique. When saying 'Ei', one forcibly expels air through vocal cords using the diaphragm. This restricts the airflow, increases air pressure in lungs and forces the oxygen into the blood stream. While in this situation the muscles are collaboratively working together, they deliver a high speed movement.

The sound **'Ya'** is often vocalized at the time of impact or often during the execution of a counter-attack or block. When saying 'Ya', one releases a burst of air from the lungs that increases pressure and tenses the entire body, especially the abdomen. When the abdomen tenses, muscles in the upper and lower body connect strongly and turn the body into a solid unit.

The sounds **'Tou'/'Hod'/Haap** are often vocalized at the delivery of the last and fatal blow or often during the execution of the final killing cut. When saying 'Tou' or 'Hod', one releases an even stronger burst of air from the lungs, and the entire body almost from head to toe gets intensified, so that the muscles can deliver the full energy with optimum Kime to the opponent. This also allows the body to transfer power completely from the legs to the point of contact and it facilitates body to transfer the reactive force quickly to the ground and back to the point of impact before termination.

Usually, immediately after 'Ya' and 'Tou', one continues with normal breathing. This disconnects the upper and lower body and the body switches into an unwind mood, helping it to quickly return to the on guard (Kamae) position. Other similar sounds that one can hear in other Martial Arts such as traditional Karate, Kenpo or Kendo etc would almost have the same effect, of course provided that they contain the right vowels to assist the air flow. Here it might be interesting to note that *normally a vocalized Kiai has 'low frequency' during the execution of technique and a 'high pitch' at the time of victory*.

Similar to a Vocal Artist (Tenor or Soprano) who applies 'vibrato' often on words with best vowels to reach out to their audience's ears, and to influence their feelings and moods, a Martial Artist also reaches out to their opponents and influences their psychology and moods with their vocalized Kiai.

Perhaps it's worth reminding that similar to music, where sometimes we have the 'silent note / rest', *we also have the **'silent Kiai'** (an internal tone) during meditation or when a technique is needed to be applied in silence*.

Could there be more scientific explanation on this matter?

Certainly. Do you remember earlier I outlined that 'Kiai' can be an INTERRUPTIVE or a DESTRUCTIVE technique? Well, here is how:

We know that sound creates 'WAVE'. Almost **70%** of our body is water. *A well-executed Kiai can create ripples in the water inside the human body. This can slow down, interrupt or even destruct the opponent.* Because Vowels could potentially create stronger sound waves, using them in Kiai could enforce the ripple in the water inside the human body.

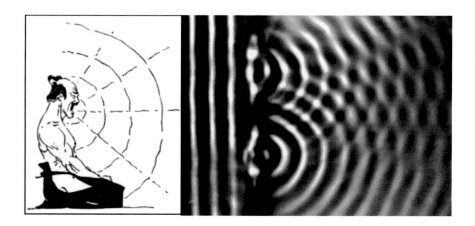

Still there is a legitimate question:

Why the vocalized sounds of Kiai in Koryu styles such as 'Katori Shinto-ryu' and its descendent branches are often different from those in Karate, Kenpo, Taekwondo, etc.?

Well, if I may say, perhaps answering this question is a very interesting part of this paper for Koryu followers especially 'Katori' practitioners. To answer this, I must say, perhaps all goes back to the method or the purpose for which a school / style or 'Ryu-ha' is created.

For example, while Martial Arts such as Kenpo, Karate, and Taekwondo are basically created for close combat with empty hands and predominantly <u>for civil self-defense</u>, the

Martial Arts such as Katori Shinto-ryu or other similar Koryu Kenjutsu styles are created predominantly <u>for battlefields</u>.

However there are close combat instructions such as Jujutsu in Katori Shinto-ryu, historically it was and still in spirit is a military school for training Samurai to fight in battles.

Therefore, one can trace the sounds of 'Ei', 'Ya', and even 'Tou'/'Hod' back to Japan's feudal area when troops, armies or clans were often fighting in battlefields.

What? The sounds are also rooted in the Battlefield?!

Well, yes!

Do you remember the second underlining definition of 'Cry'? Yes, *"a demand expressed by many people."* And do you recall, when I outlined that Kiai can also be a 'COMMUNICATIVE' technique or strategy?

Well, indeed it was a demand and a form of communication!

Usually in a battlefield as seen in the picture below, a commander cries loudly saying 'Eiii', meaning "demanding" and commanding the army to UNITE, to get together and READY for the attack. Then the clan, troop or army responds back with crying out loudly saying 'Yaaa' as the affirmation for action.[17]

So, one can imagine that 'Kiai' here has interactive or "communicative" role between the person in charge and the army under his command. While the 'Eiii' initiates, the 'Yaaa' follows through.

Chris Glenn, Author and a Samurai Historian, in his social media publication on 'The Battle of Sekigahara' writes: *"Various war cries were used at battles such as Sekigahara. The often heard "Ei Ei Ei," for three times from a commander, was an order for all to move out immediately."* On the same note for 'The Battle of Sekigahara', he mentions that *"other rallying calls of "Ei Tou Ei," and "Eiya Eiya" would have been heard across the scene of combat"*.[18]

That is why we can still hear those sounds of 'Kiai' not in the real battlefields, but in Koryu dojo, where the same spirit exists.

CONCLUSION:

While the application of Kiai (unifying energy) is almost the same in majority of Martial Arts or styles, the vocalized Kiai and its sound could be varied. Perhaps the sounds of vocalized Kiai in Gendai Budo (Modern Martial Way) is more of a personal choice and based on practitioners' self-developed skills and their instructors' level of understanding from this subject.

However, in traditional military schools of Samurai, such as Katori Shinto-ryu and its descendant schools, in addition to its application, Kiai reminds us of a sound tradition and the honor once earned in the battlefield.

Regardless of style or school, one thing is common and for certain, no matter silent or loud, '**Kiai is a cry for unity**'

PAPER 2

RIAI: MARTIAL REALITY

As I mentioned earlier, Japanese Martial Strategies are heavily influenced by Buddhism. The concept of '**Riai** 理合'is one of the aspects of martial arts rooted in that. While 'Ri' has multiple meanings, the general definition is: 'Reason' or 'Truth'. In Buddhist term, it means: *why something is 'what it is'.*

In the context of martial arts or in martial term, we can say that it is the understanding of the 'essence' of what a 'Waza / 'Kata' (Technique or Form) is. Here, perhaps some readers with Karate experience would jump into a conclusion by saying that: Oh, this is what we call 'Bunkai' (Application). But sorry, no, Riai is not Bunkai, and it is deeper than knowing how a technique works on an opponent.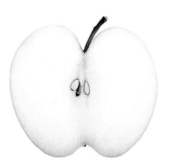

'Ri' is the essence, the reason behind the "core creation" of a technique, and the "Principle" for what it is. And of course 'Ai', as explained in the previous paper, means 'Unite'.

Allow me to explain this concept with a few different examples:

 In the practice of Aikido, there is a technique called 'Kotegaeshi' (Wrist twist). Imagine in a dojo the instructor showing his students that the opponent grabs his right wrist with right hand or both hands, and then he throws him down. Then probably once more, but this time in slow motion, and he would give an analytical explanation: when the opponent grabs your right wrist, stepping (in certain ways) while maintaining your center, you twist his wrist and force him to take a fall otherwise his wrist and elbow would be dislocated.

Now, is that step by step analytical explanation of application, 'Ri' or 'Riai'? Well, I am afraid not!

Understanding 'Ri' for techniques such as Kotegaeshi comes from series of questions. For instance:

- 'Why letting the opponent get that close to grab your wrist?'
- 'Why the right hand?'
- 'Why grabbing in the first place and not punching or kicking?'
- 'Why twisting and throwing?'
- 'Why is it done in that timing?' etc.

Now, with view to the questions above, in order to understand 'Riai' for Kotegaeshi, one would need to know **'the culture'**, **'the reason'**, and **'the essence'** for the technique.

Allow me to explain:

Aikido was founded by Ueshiba Morihei, Sensei. He was a student of Takeda Sokaku, Sensei - founder of Daito-ryu Aiki-Jujutsu School. Sokaku Sensei was also an expert in Kenjutsu (Swordsmanship). Although Ueshiba's teaching was a contemporary approach to Budo (Martial Way), his techniques and forms had an imprint from the classical martial arts such as Jujutsu and Kenjutsu.

Before the use of fire guns, people in Japan were carrying swords, and one can imagine getting attacked by a razor sharp sword was a nasty and scary thing. Therefore, logically if you are being attacked, what would be your major worry? The sword hand, right? The right hand, which draws the sword. You would grab the right hand first, neutralize it and then counter attack. If you use your left hand to neutralize his right sword hand, you will even have the chance to draw your own sword or Tanto (Knife) with your right hand and use it.

Samurai Close Combat Demo

The fear of attacker drawing his blade was the reason behind many attacks in Jujutsu, initiating with a grabbing wrist, hence practicing with a focus on the right hand, and the reason for its transmission from Aiki-Jujutsu to Aikido.

So, here you can see that just by explaining that when the opponent grabs your wrist, you turn and twist his wrist and throw him down, is rather skin-deep and unrealistic. But instead, if you look for the *'Why behind the objectives'*, and dig much deeper, you would know that why the opponent is heading to grab the wrist instead of punching in the first place. And of course in light of that, you would learn that because of its 'Principle' at the time (pre-1868), if the attacker's right hand was free, he would just draw his sword or knife and would cut or stab you to death. Also you would sense the fact that in such situations of 'life and death', correct stepping (Irimi - entering straight into a technique OR Tenkan - indirect entrance into technique), distance (Maai) and timing are crucial.

Another example for this topic could be 'Tobi Yoko Giri'. A powerful high jump / fly side-kick that one can often see in demonstrations. But does this technique have any 'Ri' beyond an impressive high jump-kick to wow the spectators? Some teachers might say, yes for example when an opponent attacks you with a Tsuki (Strait Punch), you do Sabaki (Step & Body Maneuver to get out of his direction of attack), then you jump into the air and perform the side kick to his body / neck or head. Well, isn't that yet another unrealistic description or practice?

Late Tetsuhiko Asai - Tobi Yoko Geri – Demonstration Japan 1964

Certainly it is. Perhaps here asking the 'why behind the objectives' would once again give us a better understanding on its 'Principle creation', or the 'Reason for what it is'. For instance, the first question here could be: Why jump, and why jump from the side (Yoko)?

Well, during the feudal Japan, when Warriors were ruling, Samurai had different military levels/classes, often low rankings were the foot soldiers, while the high rankings were usually mounted on horses. As a tactical strategy, some foot soldiers would take hiding behind the trees or bushes near the side roads, where the Samurai were to ride.

Then with good timing and proper distance for takeoff, they would jump into the air, perform 'Tobi Yoko Giri', and as a result dismount the Samurai from his horse.

This is therefore the reason for attacking from the side by tightly jamming the back leg under the kicking one, which gives the jumper the ability to fly over the horse back.

And of course if the attacker was short, not fully fit for a jump over or the land conditions dictated the necessity, then they would use their '**So** 槍' (Spear), or '**Bo** 棒' (Staff) to assist them for a better takeoff.

With the above description in mind, now, does it make sense to jump into the air doing 'Tobi Yoko Giri' as a counter attack to a simple Tsuki (Punch)?! Certainly not.

However this flying side kick is adopted by many martial arts and it is impressive to the eyes of people with no or less martial arts experience, when it is performed as a counter attack for a simple punch or a kick, then it is '**Muri** 無理' (Without truth) or 'not for what it is' – of course I will explain the concept of 'Muri' in detail in the next segment.

Now, here one might say, why is it so important to understand the concept of 'Riai'? Why should we try to learn the 'truth', 'reason' or 'principle', especially when we can just get by with practicing what the instructors are saying to us (the masses) in general?

Well, this depends on the individual's target. Either you want to be a true martial artist or a martial sportsman. If the latter, probably you wouldn't need to know much deeper or beyond what the competition and martial sport is requiring. However, if you want to be a true martial artist, then *you are recommended to strive for the knowledge on the 'essence' of each and every technique or form.*

Therefore, my advice to you is: <u>try to dig deeper.</u>

In my interactions with several Japanese grand masters, I often hear them say: This or that guy has no 'Ri'. So, for someone with extensive knowledge and genuine practice who has truly mastered their art, it will not take long to understand if a practitioner delivers a technique or performs a Kata simply out of habit, mechanically without the slightest clue on its principle, or out of a full understanding of its 'essence'.

Do not get me wrong, I am not saying that by repetition one cannot possibly realize the essence. Based on the individual's level of intelligence and interest, eventually they might, but I suggest in lieu of 'Ri', one had better *'practice less out of habit (mechanical) and more out of intent'*.

Martial Buddha

MURI, MURA AND MUDA:

Based on Buddhism, there is a concept called, '*Ji* 事'. *It is often an artistic or technical approach made by human to demonstrate 'Actuality'.*[19]

Similarly, in martial arts for example, a Kata (form), is an artistic and technical set of organized techniques created by human, to serve an 'actuality', i.e. a combative situation. Therefore, a Kata is ought to be realistic. Hence, it is expected to be practiced in a way that it demonstrates "the truth", "the principle", or "the essence" of its 'ACTUAL' reason for creation.

Female Performing Iai Kata

Which 'reason / actuality? **"The Martial or Combative"** ones of course.

And exactly this is one of the main reasons that many traditionalists and Koryu instructors rightfully disagree with the current methods of teaching martial arts as self-defense. Especially with regards to the teaching of Kata. These days, forms are often taught without their 'actualities', with limited attention to Bunkai - applications and certainly with limited emphasis on 'Ri'. Regretfully, the modern competitive sport, often turned them into a set of mechanical fancy and flashy movements to impress the spectators and score points.

The Author, Performing a Kojido Todi-Jutsu Kata

Also in many cases, especially in styles of Iaido, they are overly ritualized, so far so that their 'Martial' or 'Combative' aspects are lost.

Now, as briefly mentioned earlier, when one is doing the drills or Kata but has no 'Ri', then it is called "**Muri** 無理" meaning: *'Empty from essence'*, *'without principle'* or *'not being for what it is'*.

For martial artists and martial instructors, it is essential to understand both 'Ji' and 'Ri' so that during practice, they stay in the right mindset and truly martial. Otherwise, their movements would be empty and without understanding of their <u>proper intent</u>.

There are hundreds of forms and combination of techniques (new or old) out there that lack 'actuality'; therefore, practicing them inevitably produces little benefit and they are often impractical for combat or self-defense. Performing forms, techniques, and drills that in the whole or in parts are uneven and inconsistent with martial arts and its core purpose, is called '**Mura**' 斑'.

For example, when you can make a strong block with your right hand but not with your left one, when you cannot synchronize your weapon moves with your steps and body, when you are performing forms and drills, which predominantly strengthen one side of your body and not the other, or a form that emphasizes on too many defenses but limited offences, are all uneven, inconsistent and considered 'Mura'.

Here I need to emphasize that while creativity was, is and will be an essential part of martial arts dynamics, it should be done responsibly, with due diligence, and certainly with practicality in mind, based on good research, study and understanding of the situational needs. ***Creating without proper 'reason' is unstructured, and an unstructured creation is bound to collapse.***

Therefore, understanding 'Muri' and 'Mura' will help you to <u>*attentively care*</u> for what you are doing during the practice.

If you do not care for 'Ji', 'Ri', 'Muri' and 'Mura', then you most probably are 'wasting' your energy.

Here is when '**Muda** 無駄' comes into the picture. 'Muda' literally means: '*No packed horse*'. It means one has a horse and not using it!

Imagine you carrying your heavy loads on your own, while your horse is walking along with no burden!

In martial example:

Imagine your opponent moves forward to attack you with a 'Mai-giri' (front kick) but you step back too far, hence you become unable to reach him for counterattack; or your 'Irimi' (entering straight into a technique) is too slow; or your 'Taisabaki' (maneuver) is larger than needed and you are off the center; or instead of letting the gravity to assist you with your certain sword cut, you enforce it unnecessarily with shoulder muscles; or if you are only good with long sword and not with the short one.

Basically, wasting 'time', 'space', 'energy' and 'resources' are defining elements of 'Muda'.

Here, in my capacity as an executive consultant, I can confirm that these concepts of 'Muri', 'Mura', and 'Muda' are not limited to martial arts and they are being used even in manufacturing and process management: in companies such as Toyota Production System, and many German engineering, European and American industries.[20]

Similarly, in business practice, 'Muri' is 'unreasonableness' and causing stress, 'Mura' is 'inconsistency' that leads to waste and if 'Muri' and 'Mura' are not solved, what we end up with, will be 'Muda' or 'waste'. In order to increase efficiency, 'Muri', 'Mura' and 'Muda' must be eliminated from the system. This is part of '**Kaizen**' or 'Continuous Improvement' that many organizations around the world apply today.

Kai (Change)   *Zen (Good)*

Continuous Improvement

These principles are also applicable in our daily lives. With them you can analyze and examine your weaknesses and learn about your strengths; you can learn the reasons for your failures and success.

For example, if you are at work and in a business meeting, but your mind is at home, this is 'Mura'. If you promised to submit your project by Friday but it is Sunday and you are far from finishing it, this is 'Mura'.

Anything that adds burden, stress or imbalance in your life and causes you not to live your life fully, should be eliminated and those principles will help you achieve that.

Now, here the question might be: where and when there is a 'Ri' for every technique and form, what could be the 'Ri' for the very existence of martial strategy and its use by the human being?

Well, to answer this, I would rather step out of the influences of Buddhism and Shinto and look into this from the window of science. It is a fact that the Japanese martial arts are influenced by their religion, but beyond religion and / or eastern philosophy, there is a scientific fact for the core creation and the need for the fighting skills (in one form or another) for the entire human being.

FROM THE WINDOW OF SCIENCE:

Although throughout human history, most cultures have developed ideas, stories or even myths about how life and culture came into existence, the current theory of evolution, based on the ideas of 'Charles Darwin' is accepted by majority of scientists in our time.

Charles Darwin, (1809–1882) was an English Naturalist and Geologist. He is best known for his scientific contributions to evolutionary theory.[21]

Darwin's books: 'On the Origins of the Species by Natural Selection' (1859) and 'The Descent of Man' (1872), he expressed his theory of evolution and revolutionized the study of life and human origins.

Darwin presented evidence showing that natural species including humans have changed, or evolved over long spans of time. He also argued that radically new forms of life develop from existing species.

Charles Robert Darwin

He noted that all organisms compete with one another for food, space, mates, and other things needed for <u>survival and reproduction</u>.

The most successful individuals in this competition have the greatest chance of reproducing and passing these characteristics on to their offspring (survival of the fittest).

Over hundreds of thousands of generations, one form of life can evolve into one or more other forms. Darwin called this process natural selection.[22]

Now, with Darwin's theory in mind, let us review the journey that all of us took:

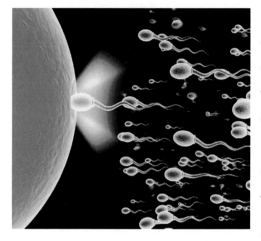

For sure most of you remember the science classes in which we learned how we were conceived and born. Here, by sharing the following writing by 'Mary Beth Clough & Ron Collins' on the process of human fertilization, I want you to pay careful attention to the underlining points and think about it with your *'martial mentality'*.

"During sexual intercourse, about <u>300 million</u> sperm enter the vagina. Soon after, <u>millions of them flow out or die in its acidic environment</u>. Many of them survive due to the protective elements that exist in the fluid surrounding them. Sperm must pass through the cervix, an opening into the uterus. Usually it remains tightly closed, but here the cervix is open for a few days while the woman ovulates.

The sperm swim through the cervical mucus, which has thinned to a more watery consistency for easier passage. Once inside the cervix, the sperm continue swimming toward the uterus, here <u>millions will die trying to make it through the mucus</u>. Some sperm remain behind, caught in the folds of the cervix, but they may later continue the journey as a backup to the first group.

Inside the uterus, muscular uterine contractions assist the sperm on their journey toward the egg. However, resident cells from the <u>woman's immune system, mistaking the sperm for foreign invaders, destroy thousands more</u>.

Next, half the sperm head for the empty fallopian tube, while the other half swim toward the tube containing the unfertilized egg. Now, <u>only a few thousand remain.</u> Inside the fallopian tube, tiny cilia push the egg toward the uterus.

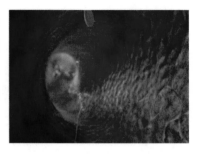

To continue, <u>the sperm must surge against the motion</u> to reach the egg. <u>Some sperm get trapped in the cilia and die.</u> During this part of journey, chemicals in the reproductive tract, cause the membrane covering the heads of sperm to change. As the result, the sperm become hyperactive, swimming harder and faster toward their destination.

At long last, the sperm reach the egg. <u>Only a few dozen of the original 300 million sperm remain.</u> The egg is covered with layer of cells called the corona radiata. <u>The sperm must push through</u> this layer to reach the outer layer of the egg, the zona pellucida. When sperm reach there, they attach to specialized sperm receptors on the surface, which triggers their acrosomes to release digestive enzymes, enabling sperm to burrow into the layer. Inside the zona pellucida is a narrow, fluid-filled space just outside the egg cell membrane. <u>The first sperm to make contact will fertilize the egg.</u>

<u>After a perilous journey and against incredible odds, a single sperm attach to the egg cell membrane.</u> With a few minutes, their outer membranes fuse, and the egg pulls the sperm inside. <u>This event causes changes in the egg membrane that prevent other sperm from attaching to it.</u>

Next, <u>the egg releases chemicals that push other sperm away from the egg and create an impenetrable fertilization membrane.</u> As the reaction spreads outwards, the zona pellucida hardens, <u>trapping any sperm unlucky enough to be caught inside.</u> Outside the egg, sperm are no longer able to attach to the zona pellucida.

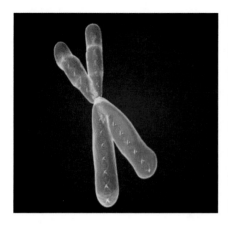

Meanwhile, inside the egg, the tightly packed male genetic material spreads out. A new membrane forms around the genetic material, creating the male pronucleus. Inside, the genetic material reforms into 23 chromosomes. The female genetic material, awakened by the fusion of sperm with the egg, finishes dividing, resulting in the female pronucleus, which also contain 23 chromosomes.

As the male and female pronucleus form spiderweb-like threads, called microtubules, pull them toward each other. The two sets of chromosomes join together, completing the process of fertilization. At this moment, a unique genetic code arises, instantly determining gender, hair color, eye color, and hundreds of other characteristics.

This new single cell, the zygote, is the beginning of a new human being. And now the cilia in the fallopian tube gently sweep the zygote toward the uterus, where s/he will implant in the rich uterine lining, growing and maturing for the nine months, until ready for birth."[23]

Now, what is your take from this journey of human fertilization to birth?

To me, it is quite clear that the very 'essence' of our creation process, be it literally or metaphorically, is based on 'SURVIVAL', and as Darwin suggests, 'survival of the fittest'. *Couldn't this be the very natural core reason for human being, needing "Survival" skills, including martial or fighting ones as part of its essential being?*

Imagine other animals: Tigers, Eagles, or Monkeys. However they need to learn how to adapt to their wild environment and to stay alive, one cannot see them learning how to fight from one another. Such animals might assist their cub, eaglet, or infant to learn how to hunt, how to fly or how to climb, but have you ever seen a tiger teach the other one how to use his intense paw in a fight? Have you ever seen  a snake or a monkey teach their kind how to bite the enemy? I haven't.

So, contrary to the human being with inferior natural fighting skills, those animals have the natural fighting capability instinctively and within their essence.

For hundreds of years, human beings have wondered and acquired how to fight with their bare hands just like those animals in order to increase their chances of survival. This led many martial arts, especially in China to adopt moves from tigers, eagles, monkeys, cranes, snakes and praying mantis. Such moves in form of various Kata, reached Okinawa and eventually became the bases for many forms being practiced today.

The Author, Performing 'Washin No Tatakai'
a Kata that depicts the fight of Eagles

Of course throwing a punch or a kick is within the natural capability of any physically sound human being and for that no particular schooling is required. And certainly since it is for thousands of years now that human race is living in various forms of civilization and less in the wild, this has changed human fighting skills and dynamics, not to mention the tactic and technology they use. But we shall not forget one important factor here and that is: **Human Intelligence!**

'The biggest challenge for human being is human being'.

To match that and survive, one needs to learn, practice and continuously improve.

According to National Geography – the fight science program: four out of five people will be the victim of at least one violent crime in their lifetime. One of the main problems is that we don't have the 'knowledge' or 'physical skill-set' to turn the situation in our favor.[24]

And it seems that for human being the need for technical and tactical advantage is in fact pre-historic.

The modern scientific study of human evolution is called 'Paleoanthropology'. It is a subfield of Anthropology, a discipline that searches for the roots of human physical traits, culture, and behavior. It attempts to answer questions such as: What is it that makes us human? When and why did we begin to walk upright? How did our brains, language, art, music, and religion develop?

Paleoanthropology shows that since human being could manipulate the objects due to the anatomy of their 'thumbs', they could develop their brain faster and use objects to create tools.[25] They could create weapons to hunt and to defend themselves against stronger species.

This manipulation of objects to create fighting and hunting weapons, indicates that:

Finding 'better', 'stronger', 'faster' techniques and tactics have always been essential for human being to survive. Human beings always need new skills, techniques and technology to give them the cutting edge or the competitive advantage.

So, here with view to Darwin's theory of life, with reference to the journey of one sperm out of 300 million and considering the facts of Paleoanthropology, I would say that **the 'Ri' for the martial arts is 'SURVIVAL'.**

The Author, Performing Okinawan Weapon (Bo, Tonfa, Sai)

Martial Strategies are created and used by human being for centuries, for one reason and one reason ONLY, to enable him to 'SURVIVE'.

'Onaga Yoshimitsu', a 77-year-old Karate master and the founder of Shinjinbukan, Okinawa - in an interviews says: *"There are times, when you mustn't lose, but it is also bad to win. What I have learned about, is this one truth in life: Competitions are about medals and winning, but life is about 'Not losing'"*.[26]

CONCLUSION:

As mentioned earlier, in my opinion, martial artists should 'strive for learning the knowledge on "the essence" of each and every technique and form'. I encourage martial artists and practitioners to ask the 'WHY behind the objectives, techniques and tactics' for at least <u>five times</u>, and make sure the answer to each would provide a deeper layer of understanding.[27]

Here some teachers might say, students should be ready before being told 'Why'. True, but are you sure you are not using this as an excuse for not admitting that perhaps you don't know or you don't feel it necessary to find out and share? Certainly there must be a level of maturity for full comprehension on the objectives, BUT, *curiosity must be there too and fully encouraged among the students. Especially, if they're expected to learn well, and pass on the traditions.*

As for the practice, in my view, whilst it is possible to practice safe, it is equally possible to train with proper degree of intensity and passive resistance, which will make one more effective in the real situation. It is absolutely possible to train safely, without cheating on techniques or reducing their martial values.

I believe, **'Intent' influences 'Action', which influences 'Result'.**

Training that contains 'Muri', 'Mura' and 'Muda' will not produce well and will eventually lead you to failure.

The secret science of 'Riai' is:

1. To understand and accept that our very core life is about 'Surviving';
2. To 'Survive', we must eliminate 'Inefficiencies';

3. To have efficiency, we need to 'unify principles', that is to unite 'Reason, Essence, Theory, and Culture' with 'Practice'.

Therefore to me, **'Riai, is martial reality.'**

This is brushed by the author, it depicts a Batto-Jutsu Kata: 'Yukiai Gyakunuki No Tachi'

PAPER 3

UKE: A BLESSED RECEIVER

'Uke 受け*'* is often described as 'block' or 'defense'. While this may be a close interpretation, it is certainly broader and needs a deeper analysis. The correct meaning and the concept of 'Uke' can be searched in its Kanji. 'Uke' literally means '**Receiving**'.

If you carefully look at its Kanji, it illustrates two arms, one reaching downward, and the other upward, and in the middle the character for 'boat' is allotted. This shows shipping goods from one person to another, which depicts the action of 'receiving'.

In martial arts often the person who 'receives' a technique is called 'Uke', but in pair work and partner drills the role of 'Uke' is varied from style to style. For example, in Aiki-Jujutsu or Tai-Jutsu the person who initiates an offensive technique is the 'Uke', and as the result of their initiation, they 'receive' an offensive or counter attack technique. In Karate, the one being attacked is 'Uke' or 'Ukete', the receiving hand. In Kendo and Kenjutsu the 'Ukedachi' is the receiving sword.

In Jujutsu and other similar grabbling arts, the action of 'Uke' is called '**Ukemi** 受け身', literally meaning '*Passive*' but in the martial term it means the 'Receiving Body' and this is absolutely an active physical process.

In any pair work practice, the role of 'Uke' is very important. Because 'Uke' must know how to react precisely, correctly and timely, and apply skills to facilitate a continuance, safe practice and development. The concept of 'Uke' can be analyzed in various ways, but in order to describe it strategically, one needs to consider:

'Mass', 'Mobility / Maneuver' and 'Mentality of Defense'. Let me explain more:

MASS, MOBILITY AND MENTALITY OF DEFENSE:

Often when I look at Japanese Castles, similar to the picture below, I am reminded of their true purpose. They were built to be a fortress and primarily to serve military defense.

Kumamoto Castle located in Chuo-ku, Kumamoto Prefecture

Japanese castles were often built on top of hills or on natural or man-made mounds. This was mainly to reinforce the defense capabilities and facilitate a greater view over the surroundings, not to mention that it made the castle appear more majestic and intimidating to invade. They were often built to manifest power and authority.

The stone walls beneath such castles are called '***Musha-gaeshi*** 武者返し' meaning 'Warriors rebuff'.

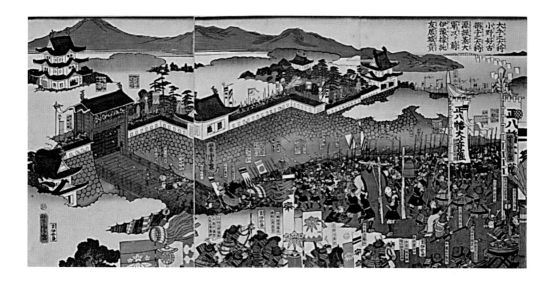

From strategic military point of view, let us imagine an attack occurs to such a castle. Warriors from outside start throwing arrows. While some may hit targets, many arrows would hit those masses of Musha-gaeshi or the thick wall shields. Although they might scratch or at best crack the stones, they would not penetrate through.

The masses of stone walls would tolerate the punishment. Due to the physical structure and type of material, those stone walls and shields could '*receive*' and stand against arrows and *there is no need for 'mobility / maneuver' for a solid structure in order to resist such direct attacks*.

As for the Warriors inside the castle, they would be protected to some extent by those tall stone walls and thick wooden shields. Hence *with limited concern about their physical mobility,* they are able to focus on their response and counterattacks simply because the forces of the attack and their level of punishments are absorbed by the walls, stones and shields and not by the human body.

The Warriors outside the castle however, *must be very concerned about their 'mobility, maneuver and how to defend themselves'*. They are more vulnerable at the time of counterattack. Since human body can tolerate only certain degrees of punishment and pain, they need to be absolutely cautious about their 'defense' or 'block' mechanism, because their *'receiving'* tolerance is way lower than a solid stone, or a thick wooden shield for example.

Now let us just imagine that the enemies could eventually climb up and get through the gate and inside the castle. You are now in a close range combat situation. What would your 'defense mentality' tell you? How would your body react? Wouldn't mobility, maneuver, and type of block become critical at this point?

Well, here is when your defense mechanism depends on whether you are 'armed' or 'unarmed' and on how you were strategically trained for close combat situations.

Of course you would want to fight to death with honor, but in order to keep fighting, you would need to stay resistant and alive. So, the very first thing that your 'Defense Mentality' would dictate you is most probably *'Surviving'*.

Now, based on the 'surviving' mentality, and the degree of your 'will', you would apply your logic to defend yourself. *Your 'defense mentality', 'physical ability', 'fighting skills' and 'experience' will navigate you when to initiate an attack, do a block or a counterattack, to suit you best to survive.*

Now let us imagine one of those invaders is facing you. Both of you are armed with your 'Katana – Sword', and both equally and fully capable of offense and defense. Here which one would be your priority: 'attacking first' or 'avoiding opponent's attack'?

Since you are both equally armed and any attack could result in a serious injury or even death, logically you would give priority to 'avoiding the opponent's attack'; therefore, your *'mobility and type of block' become important.*

Now imagine during this fight, your opponent gets lucky and somehow your Katana falls from your hand. He then has superiority and a killing weapon, and you are unarmed and empty-handed. Here is when *'mobility and type of block' become imperative.*

And just for the sake of argument, let's imagine the above scenario was the other way around, i.e. you got lucky and your opponent is now empty-handed and unarmed. What would you do?

Well, in my view, *'never, ever underestimate an empty-handed warrior, who is equally determined to survive!'*

Disarming Opponent with Empty Hand

To understand the strategy and science of 'Uke' you need to remember a couple of points in 'Physics'. Points such as 'Momentum' and 'Force'. In the next segment, I will briefly review them.

MOMENTUM AND FORCE:

Momentum is a term in physics; it refers to the quantity of motion that an object has. An opponent that is on the move has the momentum. If an object or weapon is in motion (on the move) then it has momentum. Momentum can be defined as "mass in motion." All objects have mass, so if  an object is moving, it has its mass in motion. The amount of momentum that an object has, depends upon two variables: *'how much the object is moving' and 'how fast it is moving'*. Momentum depends upon the two variables of mass and velocity. In terms of an equation, the momentum of an object is equal to the mass of the object times the velocity of the object. **Momentum** = Mass x Velocity.

Momentum measures the 'motion content' of an object. Momentum doubles, for example, when velocity doubles. Similarly, if two objects are moving with the same velocity, one with twice the mass of the other also has twice the momentum.

Force, on the other hand, is the push or pull that is applied to an object to *'Change'* its momentum. *Newton's second law of motion defines force as the product of mass times 'Acceleration' vs Velocity.*

Since acceleration is the change in velocity divided by time, you can connect the two concepts with the following relationship:

Force = mass x (velocity / time) = (mass x velocity) / time = momentum / time
Multiplying both sides of this equation by time: Force x time = momentum

The difference between 'force' and 'momentum' is **'TIME'**.

With view to the description of 'physics', the crucial point for 'receiver' is **'TIME'**.

'The use of 'Least' amount of energy, to create the 'Most' amount of force to deal with an attack in TIME'.

So, in martial strategy, in the one hand *'positioning', movement' and maneuver'* would be important and on the other hand the *'timing'*.

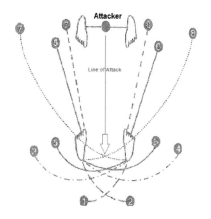

In *'**Gungaku Heiho** 軍学兵法'* (Martial Strategies) or even in *'**Gunji Enshu** 軍事演習'* (Military Exercises) there is a major emphasis on both *'positioning'* and *'timing'* for the defense.

In military science, there is a concept for 'defense positioning', which is called: *'**Gunji Dakkyu** 軍事脱臼* (Military Misplacement); in martial arts it is known as

*'**Tai-Sabaki** 体捌き or Sabaki'* (Body Shifting / Body Maneuver). That is, by *'moving out of the line of attack, you misplace the attacker, causing them to miss their target'.*

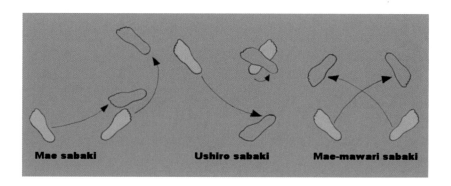

Mae sabaki   **Ushiro sabaki**   **Mae-mawari sabaki**

But defense is also being practiced in terms of 'timing'. And for that you need to know the types of initiatives.

STRATEGIC TYPES OF INITIATIVES:

In Japanese martial arts, '*Sen* 先' means 'Initiative', and it is a decisive moment when a killing action is initiated.

- '*Sen No Sen* 先の先' (Early initiative);
- '*Go No Sen* 後の先' (Late initiative);
- '*Sensen No Sen* 先先の先' (Anticipative / Preemptive initiative).

Sen No Sen: After you recognize the attacker's intention, you initiate before their attack reaches you.

Go No Sen: After you see the actual attack, you respond (with a block or other techniques).

Sensen No Sen: After you recognize the attacker's intention to attack, you deal with the attacker *before his intention becomes an attacking move.*

For a beginner in martial arts, 'Uke' is a simple reaction of block to an attack. But to more advanced practitioners, it is a secret strategy to gain superiority. Of course in any fight, one would like to defend, and at the same time, to have tactical advantage. In order to have tactical advantage, one would need to apply the above initiatives. Here, one might say but the initiatives are offensive, how come they are considered as defense?

Well, by reducing your opponent's capability, you are actually defending yourself.

Moving out of the line of attack and causing misplacement, is a 'positioning defense', a type of block which is not always possible. Therefore, the initiation in the manners of 'Sen No Sen', 'Go No Sen' or 'Sensen No Sen', are actually blocks in 'timing' through which, the capability of your opponent is affected.

In martial strategies, a block can be an attack or an attack can be a block at the same time. It depends how you would want to 'receive' or perceive it!

Let us look at this in more details.

CHARACTRESTICS OF UKE:

In principle, a 'receiver' can apply the followings, based on their strategy for defense:

Age-Uke: Upward block
Edina & Karoly Dany, Yudansha of Kojido

- **'Rakka** 落花**'** (Falling Petals): *Blocking with such force and precision as to completely destroying the opponent's attacking motion and confidence. Imagine if it was applied on the trunk of a tree, it would drop its flowers.*

- **'Ryusui** 流水**'** (Flowing Water): Flowing around the attacker's motion, and through it: a soft blocking. Using the opponent's movement for fluid defense, i.e. absorbing the attack and re-directing it using circular or deflecting blocks.

- **'Kusshi** 屈伸**'** (Elasticity): Bouncing out and in, bending and stretching, controlling the opponent's attack, using flexible body movement generated from the knee, and changing or lowering stance only to immediately unwind and counterattack.

- **'Ten i** 転位**'** (Transposition): Utilization of all eight directions of movement, more importantly stepping out of the line of attack (Tai-Sabaki).

- **'Hangeki** 反撃**'** (Counterattack): An attack which at the same time deflects the opponent's attack before it can reach the defender (Go No Sen).

For further understanding of 'Uke' and its applications, one needs to equally pay attention to 'Space'. In the following segment let us look at 'space and distance'.

ENGAGEMENT DISTANCE:

Maai 間合い literally means *'Interval'*. It makes reference to the space between opponents in a combat. In Shobun Heiho (individual martial strategy), it is the *'Engagement Distance'*.

It is a complex notion and it blends 'time' as well.

Maai for close range unarmed combat in Kojido

'Maai' is not only a concept for distance (space) but also the time it takes to cross the distance, rhythm and angle of the attack.

'Tactically, it is the best distance to attack faster' and *'strategically, it is the distance you need to maintain while preventing your opponent from doing so'*. The farther your opponent in their 'Maai', the slower their attack and the easier for you to counter.

Generally 'Maai' can be:

- **'Toi-maai 遠い'** (Long distance): Space that takes more than one step to strike the opponent.

- **'Issoku-itto-no-maai 一足'** (Short distance): Space that takes one step to strike the opponent *(Height is important here. The taller opponent's one step Maai will be longer)*

- **'Chikai-maai 近い'** (Close distance): space closer than one step to strike the opponent.

Of course further to this topic, in the following papers I will discuss one of the most strategic forms of defense as well as the science of movements and the state of mind.

CONCLUSION:

'Uke' is beyond a block, it is the attitude of 'receiving'. It is an active process that requires one to flow, to absorb, to fall, to block, to throw, to counter, to react, to interact, to intercept, to calculate, to control and to maintain.

In a dojo during practice, *the person who does the 'Uke' has a nurturing, facilitating, and developing role.* In pair work drills, *'Uke' is expected not to be so soft to spoil or overly harsh to discourage. While 'Uke' has a passive resistance, their action must not be stubborn.*

'Uke' must maintain a high level of mental stability and an esteemed physical endurance. In martial strategies, you should remember that if you have to think about a very sophisticated and difficult block, it might not be there when you really need it.

For easier and faster counter, you are recommended to keep your blocks and deflects simple. *Depending on your combative situation and strategy, you need to remember that it is not just how fast you block, it is how fast you get out of the line of attack and if necessary counter!* **You should always be aware of your opponent's rhythm and speed.**

Blocking with hands, arms or with your Sword's *'Shinogi'* (Blade Ridge) or deflecting with *'Mune'* (Back of Blade) are like branches of a tree. While they are extended to defend you, your body should stay strongly like a tree and **you should always maintain your center of gravity.** Practicing Uke, if done with positive attitude is advantageous, hence it makes one to be **'a blessed receiver'**

PAPER 4

HYOSHI: A RYHTHM OF RISE OR FALL

In the previous paper I mentioned that the difference between 'Force' and 'Momentum' is 'Time', and I wrote that 'Maai'- Distance is a complex notion, which blends 'time' and 'rhythm' as well. In martial arts, it is almost impossible to speak about 'Maai' and not address its dimension of 'Rhythm'.

Oxford Dictionary defines 'Rhythm' as: "A strong, regular repeated pattern of movement or sound" and in 'Biorhythm' term as: "A cyclic pattern of physical, emotional or mental activity believed to occur in a person's life". In this respect, the body clock and the understanding of physiological parameters of the human circadian rhythm in roughly 24 hours becomes important. It not only scientifically recommends the best timing for human activities, but also suggests how to best plan for engaging in an activity for a favorable result. This study of human circadian rhythm can be of use for martial arts training, combats and field operations or even normal daily life activities.

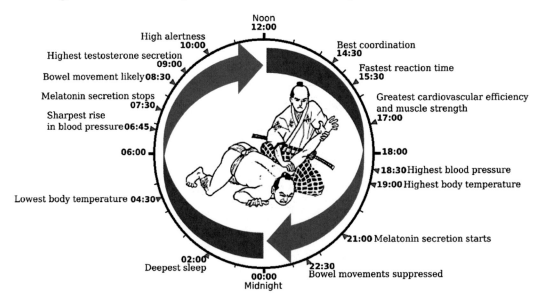

In the 'Performing art' however, rhythm is the timing of events on a human scale; of musical sounds and silences, of the steps of a dance, or the length of spoken language and poetry.

Japanese Sword Dance

Bu No Mai: Okinawan Martial Dance with Sai

While rhythm can be found in many things, in martial arts it can be understood best through extensive training. In martial context, rhythm is a combination of the 'pattern of movement' and the 'cyclic emotion and mentality', which occurs during the 'time' of an event.

In martial arts, no movement is without rhythm. Every movement has both 'physical' and 'mental' rhythm. Even when you appear still and motionless, your muscles are contracting and relaxing and you are breathing; therefore, you have rhythm attached to your next movement in the making.

In combat, you live each moment surrounded by the series of rhythm. '**Hyoshi** 拍子' (Rhythm / Beat / Tempo) is a complex term in Japanese culture. *It is a rhythmic spatiotemporal intervals (space-time) produced mutually not only between the two fighters but also at the very same time to the tempo of each of them, which is closely related to each fighter's* breathing *and* mental state.

Therefore we can say that *the perspicacity or experience of timing and rhythm of combat is not set like a music sheet, it is not unified, nor is it easy to detect. It is often unpredictable.* Before going to the combative, strategic and scientific details, and to better understanding the concept of 'Hyoshi', first let us examine the Japanese culture of 'Hyoshi' through the art of the 'Tea Ceremony':

THE CONCEPT OF HYOSHI IN JAPANES CULTURE:

Dr. Inazo Nitobe (1862 -1933), Agriculturalist, Philosopher, Statesman, and Educator writes: *"The art of drinking tea is a poem that draws its rhythm from harmonious movements"*[28]

The Japanese tea ceremony is called '**Chanoyu** 茶の湯', '**Sado** 茶道'. It is a choreographic ritual of preparing and serving Japanese powdered green tea (Matcha), together with traditional Japanese sweets to balance with the bitter taste of the tea. Where tea leaf (Sencha) is used, the ceremony is addressed as '**Senchado** 煎茶道'. The art of its performance is called '**Temae** 手前', and it is influenced by 'Zen Buddhism'. Preparing tea in this ceremony means pouring all one's attention into the predefined movements. The Tea Master (host of the ceremony) always muses the guests with every movement and gesture. Even the placement of the tea vessel/tools is laid out for the guests' best view angle and visual scene.

During the 'Tea Ceremony', the tea master, who prepares the tea and the guest, who drinks it both pass the time of the ceremony within a pre-arranged space and each perform certain movements, which indicate a mental state of harmony. So both participants move in 'time and space'. For those who are watching the ceremony from outside, the activities of the tea master and the guest are the rhythmic harmonious movements of the tea ceremony. That is, water is heated, tea is prepared, then it is offered with utmost respect, and the guest receives it with proper manner and drinks it.

In order for the tea to be drunk properly, each participant's movements, their mental and emotional state, and even their way of existence in a given space must harmonize perfectly with the space and time and when this occurs, we can say the rhythm is created.

Here the rhythm is totally interpersonal. There is an inter-relation between the tea master and the guest, as well as their audience or other attendees. Here a 'Hyoshi' or rhythm is established among the tea master, the guest and their audience.

Notably, one should remember that 'Hyoshi' is created by using objects (kettle, tea bowl, tea scoop, tea whisk etc.) as well as their entire environment. In the Japanese culture, it is literally through entering into a relationship with objects that a rhythm is established and it is that rhythm that makes human to enter into harmony with other human or with the nature.

Therefore it is capital to understand that in the Japanese culture, objects are not dissociated from the rhythm of life.

Now with having the "Cultural" understanding of rhythm, let us attend the 'combative' and 'strategic' aspects of rhythm and tempo in martial arts.

SECRET AND SICENCE OF RHYTHM IN MARTIAL STRATEGY:

Similar to the 'Tea Ceremony', where the tea masters, their utensils, resources and their environment are all inclusive, in martial strategy, the martial artists are not separated from their weapons, resources and combative environment. As tea ceremony students can become more skilled by using their utensils regularly, improve their performances and eventually become tea masters, so can martial artists excel in using their body, weapons, techniques and tactics and eventually become skilled strategists.

The Way of Tea - The Way of Sword

Like tea masters, who must first learn about their tools, materials, and techniques and then use them to perform a tea ceremony, martial artists must first learn about their body, weapons as well as techniques prior to applying them in action.

So, for martial artists, the learning and developing begin with physical training, knowing their body, their weapons, and how their body and weapons can work in harmony. Once they progressed and learnt how to use their body and weapons, they can enter the next stage, which is applying what they learnt or practiced. It will be during the application of techniques when one would realize whether what they do is actually working or needs adaptation. Here comes the time, when a martial artist will learn how to adapt, adjust and change their course of actions where and when necessary.

In most cases, adapting, adjusting and changing courses of action is due to the 'Hyoshi –
Rhythm' of the event (inclusive of your own, your opponent and your environment).
Rhythm changes you, it organizes and synchronizes your brain to its beat.

In '***Go Rin No Sho*** 五輪書' (The Book of Five Rings) written by Miyamoto Musashi, Ronin
(1584 – 1645) we come across his view on rhythm, which is described as following:

"Within the rhythm of large and small, fast and slow, you should understand the rhythm
of striking, the rhythm between actions, and the use of counter rhythms."

While Musashi's explanation of strategy of rhythm is stellar, it has plenty of room for
various interpretations and might not be very clear for less advanced martial artists.

For a clearer understanding, let me give you another example from the Japanese tea
ceremony and then come back to what Musashi is trying to say:

If a tea master rushes in tea preparation, or is too slow in making it, the tea would be
either unpleasant or too cold to drink. If a tea master does not care about the layout,
arrangement of utensils, the distance and angles, and seating positions, the presentation
and reception will be out of harmony.

In the one hand we have the rhythm for 'Space', the distance of which will be paved in
time, and in the other hand we have 'Time', which is passed in pace (fast or slow motion).

A martial artist must consider the 'Space' (large or small/ far or close) and 'Time' (fast or
slow) in a combative event. If you are stepping too close or too far, or you can't control
your opponent's distance or space, you may put yourself in danger. If you act out of hurry
and too fast or in the contrary too slow, or too early or too late, you may as well put
yourself at risk.

You have to fully grasp your rhythm as well as your opponent's rhythm in both terms of 'Space and Time'. *Similar to the 'tea ceremony', where all parties try to be in harmony by attending the rhythm, in martial arts the same harmony must be found but for a different purpose.*

Every combative situation has a sequence of 'attack', 'counterattack', 'action in between' and 'moving on to the next sequence or change'. Every still or motion part of those sequences has a rhythm created by physical, emotional, and mental states.

And I believe Musashi is trying to point out those, i.e. 'the timing for attack', 'the timing to counter', 'the action in between the attack and counter' the 'change of mood' all with the consideration of 'space'.

Earlier I mentioned that *'the experience of timing and rhythm of combat is not something unified and that it is unpredictable'*. I believe the emphasis and warning on its ***'unpredictability'*** is right in front of us, and we just need to look carefully at the kanji characters for 'Hyoshi'. In my view, the secret of martial rhythm is hidden in its kanjis.

The first kanji character '**Hyo** 拍' along with its phonetic corresponds *'hands tapping'* and the second kanji character '**shi** 子' depicts a *'child'*. How does a child tap or clap? Often a child's way of tapping and clapping is irregular, in another word it is 'unpredictable'.

As the kanji characters for 'Hyoshi' suggests, the challenge is: *reading and seeing what is 'unpredictable'*; therefore, in combative situations you need to be watchful and mentally present to find harmony and attack when there is a void in your opponent's rhythm. 'Unpredictability' applies to you too; you need to maintain your 'unpredictability' so that it makes it harder for your opponent to read you. That is, while you are staying 'unpredictable', you should be able to 'predict' your opponent and read them inside-out.

Finding harmony while staying unpredictable but predicting your opponent's move, ALL at the same time, requires years of training and mental practice.

The sequence of techniques largely depends on establishing rhythm of movement regulated by mental projection and the physical sensation of the martial artist. The set of movements such as attacks, counters, blocks, body shifting, etc. are provoked concurrently by <u>breathing</u> and the <u>muscular tensions</u>.

Although based on skills and capabilities the breathing and flow of muscular tensions are varied from opponent to opponent and it is hard to read, *the teaching and practicing of martial arts must be in such a way that facilitates practitioners to develop skills to read and to see the opponent's Hyoshi.*

The key secret in maintaining 'Maai' – Distance (Interval), both in terms of 'space and time' is finding the rhythm of your opponent and establishing a harmony that enables you to find a void in their rhythm.

In this subject, I would highly recommend my readers to study and consult the publications of 'Kuroda Tetsuzan, Soke'. [29] His unique movements, is described as: **"moving in the gaps and spaces of opponent's mind".**

Now that you learnt about 'Hyoshi' from various aspects, the question might be, how to improve and excel in it. Well, if you remember I mentioned that ***every movement has both 'physical' and 'mental' rhythm and*** <u>***they are connected to breathing.***</u>

By knowing how breathing affects your heart, brain and therefore your rhythm, you will be equipped with the knowledge to build up your skills.

'Tom Seabourne', PhD – Specialist in strength and conditioning explains[30]:

"Breathing is subtle, yet quite extraordinary. It takes mindfulness to find it. And although breathing is normally involuntary, an act of will can slow it down or speed it up; make it long and diaphragmatic, or short and thoracic. Breathing is a present-time, mindful process. It is always happening, right now. You cannot be fondling memories or planning your future when you're contemplating your breath. Observe your breath, and you are automatically in the present. You are in the here-and-now.

One breathing strategy is to pay attention to the sensations as air passes through your nostrils. Inhale through your nose. Notice the point just inside your nose where you have the most powerful sensation of air flow. Exhale and feel the sensation again. Focus your attention on this spot. Use this single point to keep your attention fixed.

Don't try any specific breathing techniques. Just watch your breath. Although you control the pace of your inhalation-exhalation cycle, let your breathing proceed at its natural pace. Sometimes it slows or speeds up, and sometimes it is deep, short, or choppy. Just observe. And watch how thoughts inadvertently affect your breathing. Each time though, come back to the object of your focus—your breath.

At the beginning of your inhalation, follow your breath just for that inhalation. Then, at the start of your exhalation, follow your breath just for that exhalation. Focus on a single breath cycle. Forget about the last breath, and don't think about the next one.

There are a variety of psychological and physiological factors that affect your heart rate. The pace of your heart is unique to your body. It is self-regulating. You don't have to do a thing and it keeps beating. It maintains its own rhythm to keep you alive. But your hormonal responses and your central nervous system (CNS) and autonomic nervous system (ANS) can affect the speed and rhythm of your heart. Your hormones send chemicals into your blood to affect your heart's pace.

And your heart beats faster or slower depending on how your nerves stimulate your heart. While reading this passage, imagine your spouse or a good friend tapping you on your shoulder. External input from your nerves and hormones automatically increase your heart rate. Or, think back to when you were driving your car and somebody cut you off. Your heart raced uncontrollably although you were just sitting quietly (or not so quietly).

Mindfulness allows you to predict and override a conditioned physiological response—that is, it allows you to regulate your heart rate when you are threatened and to handle any situation appropriately.

The medulla of your brain is your control center for your heart rate. It either speeds or slows your beats per minute. Your ANS has two components: Your sympathetic nervous system (SNS) and parasympathetic nervous system (PNS). Your SNS speeds your heart rate by releasing hormones and chemicals called norepinephrine, epinephrine, and catecholamine. When your heart rate increases to a frenzy this is termed tachycardia. There are no

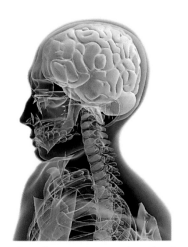

cardiovascular benefits when your sympathetic nervous system increases your heart rate. It is simply your hormones sending stimulating chemicals to your heart, and nerves directly affecting your heart to respond to an emergency.

Your PNS is in your brain stem. This is the area that slows your heart rate. A chemical that your PNS releases to slow your heart rate is called acetylcholine. When your heart rate slows, you experience bradycardia. Yogis can slow their heart rates to the less than 20 beats per minute (BPM). And the famous magician, 'Harry Houdini' was able to survive in a coffin-sized airtight box for hours.

Your nerves and hormones together regulate your heart rate when you are moving, and when you are still. As you begin training, your heart rate speeds up because your PNS is inhibited. That is, the mechanisms that slow your heart are essentially turned off, and your BPM naturally increases. Other factors besides exercise that affect the pace of your heart include blood sugar levels, different foods, lack of sleep, anxiety, fear, and anger. Chronic nervousness, sometimes referred to as "trait anxiety" can cause your heart rate to remain elevated for extended periods.

If you are tired, on medication, under stress, at high altitude, or in high humidity, your heart rate may change. Therefore, be mindful of environmental factors."

CONCLUSION:

In martial arts, the strategy is: while you try to find your own 'Hyoshi', you should seize and apprehend that of your opponent, then find a deprivation or preferably a void in your opponent's rhythm by relying on the harmony that you established between you and your opponent .

You need to master your skills and refine your techniques and tactics in such a way that you are able to manipulate 'space' 'time' and 'rhythm' against your opponent and act in harmony. So much so that when your opponent moves, your reaction is overpowering rapidly and swiftly like a thunderstorm. When you are on halt, your opponent must go through a distressful agonizing stillness that cannot resist to rush exposing an opening, which results in their defeat.

In maintaining 'Maai' and recognizing 'Hyoshi', you need to pay careful attention to 'Breathing' as well as every single tiny movements that your opponent makes including their blinking while masking your own mind and body.

Moreover, *your victory is also determined by how you mentally see the distance between you and your opponent. You need to have great confidence, mental presence and see yourself dominant and not inferior.* That is what your mentality should project and that is the way you should carry yourself.

Since in martial strategy such notion is decisive, **'Hyoshi, is a rhythm of rise or fall'**

PAPER 5

KO BO ICHI: A STRATEGIC MERGER

In the previous paper, I concluded that the very essence of life is about 'survival', hence the need for martial skills among others. In this paper, I will highlight one of the most effective and strategic techniques and tactics in martial arts and try to address it from the **'Psychological'** point of view. I will also briefly discuss the importance of the 'Psychology of Survival' in martial arts.

'*Ko Bo Ichi* or *Kogeki Bobi* 攻撃 防備' literaly means '*Offense and Defense are one*'. This can also be traced in the concept in 'Kyo-Jitsu' (Duality) based in Inyo or Yin and Yang, which I will describe in the next paper. There are very many examples that could illustrate this, as well as the tactical strategy behind it. For example: **'Kiri Otoshi Men'** a dropping downward cut to the head, while deflecting the sword, which can be seen in the school of 'Ono-ha Itto-ryu' Kenjutsu (Swordsmenship) or similarly in style of 'Kendo'.

Yano Sensei, Teaching 'Men Kiri Otoshi Men' with Bokken

Or the various **'Uke'** blocks in Karate, Kenpo, and Taijutsu, which can not only deflect attacks but at the same time break the attacker's body and cause serious damage or collapse to reduce the opponents' offensive approach.

Sawari sensei - Nippon Kenpo, Performing Kobo Ichi

Yagyu Shingan-ryu Taijutsu Demo At Meiji Shrine

However normally the 'Offense' and 'Defense' are two separate entities, *where and when the 'space' and 'time' get narrower and shorter, they both get closer and eventually merge as one.*

Often pictures in magazines and books portray a sequence of 'Block-Pause-Counterattack', a sort of 'one-two' rhythm. Or in movies, we see that the bad guy simply stands perplexed after his initial attack is deflected by the protagonist. But the fact of the matter is that *in martial strategy a 'one-two' rhythm is not effective*!

Vosoughi Sensei of Kojido, Performing 'Suri Uke'- Sliding Block & Attack as one

In reality, as soon as you block an attack, your opponent will engage to strike another attack before you launch your counterattack. Therefore, if you choose to use the 'one-two' rhythm, then you will always be on the defense.

Hiji Uke - Elbow block

'Ko Bo Ichi' is not about 'block – pause – counterattack'. Such 'one-two' rhythm is often instructed to beginners to master both offense and defense techniques. In advanced levels and in reality, this is a block that is intended to make the attacker imbalanced, to collapse, and to feel pain or damage.

Why? *In order to force him to change his offensive approach to a defensive one.*

In performing 'Ko Bo Ichi', 'proper timing', 'subtle body shifting' and 'mental fortitude' are crucial. But why am I highlighting 'Ko Bo Ichi / Kogeki Bobi' and 'Psychology' here?

Well, perhaps you are familiar with this saying:

"He who hesitates, is dead!"

If you are an experienced martial artist, for sure there were times when you told yourself: 'Darn, I should have attacked first', or 'I should have blocked stronger', or 'I should have manuvered faster' etc.

Well, in a dojo you can always get back to practice more and improve, BUT in the real world, in a nasty street, or a tough neiborhood, you probobly only have the one chance. Either your action or block would save your life or it will give your foe the chance to engage in more attacks.

<u>**However confrontation and engagement in a fight should always be avoided**</u>, *where and when it is the last resort and your life is at risk, then your block must not be just a defensive mechanism, but an offensive one at the very same time.*

'Ko Bo Ichi' is one of those tactics that many forms of Japanes martial art schools apply in their practices, and in my view, it has the best strategic approach as far as the real combative situation is concerned.

Moreover, practicing techniques based on 'Ko Bo Ichi' requires: 'flexibility', 'attention', 'awareness', 'timing', 'speed', and above all the 'mental strength'. *'Ko Bo Ichi' not only teaches us 'not to be hesitant', but also facilitates the exercise of 'Psychology of Survival'.*

THE PSYCHOLOGY OF SURVIVAL:

It is simply true that some people with limited or no survival self-defense practice have managed to survive life-threatening circumstances, while some others with training have not used their skills and lost their lives.

How many Samurai died, simply because they hesitated for an instant? How many people in our time are hospitalized because they could not defend themselves against an assault? And of course, how many could avoid confrontation or a fight and reach their destination safely?

Well, in my view, the key is **'The Mental Attitude'** of the person involved in such situations.

Having the survival skills and self-defense techniques are important, BUT having the will to survive is absolutely essential! That is why there is a "psychology" behind it.

The 'psychology of survival' is relevant, when one is situated in a hostile, combative, and life-threatening environment.

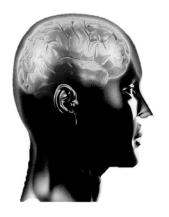

When one is in a surviving situation, they often experience stress. This will impact their mind and such stresses can lead to thoughts, emotions and worries, which can easily change a very confident well-trained person to an 'indecisive' and 'inefficient' individual.

Dr. A. R. Roberts performed a psychological study in 2000, which he reported in his 'Crisis Intervention Handbook'.[31]

He noted these common reactions in the midst of a crisis:

- "People first begin to recognize that there is a threat.
- Next, these individuals discover that the stress and trauma of the event cannot be dealt with using existing coping skills.
- People then begin to experience fear, confusion, and stress.
- Those facing a crisis begin to exhibit symptoms of distress and discomfort.
- Finally, people enter a state of imbalance, where the crisis situation seems insurmountable."

With view to the above, Daisy Luther, author of 'In All Prepping', in an article on psychology of survival writes: "During military training, recruits are put into situations that train them to immediately assess a situation and instantly choose a course of action. This allows them to act more quickly than other people, and it gives them an advantage in many scenarios. One way to do that is by skipping the cognitive-dissonance phase.

You must go through the reactions [outlined above] quickly or not at all in order to respond quickly. If you can immediately accept that something out of the ordinary has occurred, you will be able to move on to the assessment phase instead of wasting precious reaction time convincing yourself that the event itself has occurred."[32]

HOW TO SPEED UP OUR REACTIONS IN UNEXPECTED SITUATIONS?

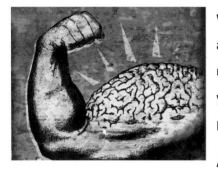

Well, here you need to work both on your 'physical' and 'mental' power and skills. On the one hand, you need to physically exercise well, and on the other, you need to have 'the mental attitude' or 'the mental preparation' facing such circumstances'.

As mentioned in the previous paper, your physical exercise must prepare you for the reality, and not just for a modern martial sport event, which often is limited to a few minutes of contest.

Your physical training must have a reasonable degree of intensity and passive resistance that puts you in the right mind set, facing hundreds of scenarios that might occur in real situations.

A type of training that increases your speed of *'assessment', 'decision making'* as well as *'physical reactions'*. The timing between 'the mental processing of the situation', 'decision making' and 'physical execution' of your technique must be reduced to a split of a second.

Please note that in real situations, 'fear' is involved and your 'adrenaline' level will increase, which will certainly affect your skills and mental state. Today, there are many people who only train for tournaments and not for saving their life. If training for self-defense is your goal, then <u>you are supposed to train for the fight that you don't want to do and try to avoid.</u>

To achieve that, similar to a military soldier, who attends combat stimulating programmes or combat virtual reality, you need to practice the *"martial reality"*.

And here comes the core reason for highlighting 'Ko Bo Ichi': Where and when, the space and time is narrow and short, when your opponent is with his maximum aggression, when in comparison to your opponent you are smaller, shorter or lighter, then the application of techniques based on 'Ko Bo Ichi' can be favorable and life-saving. How so?

Well, *psychologically speaking, to survive a life-threatening situation, you have to 'synchronize your mind and body as one', and as fast as possible; therefore, you would be better off if you 'merge your offense and defense as one' too. In this way, you save even more precious time.*

A powerful block that could hurt too –
Defense and Offense as one

CONCLUSION:

'Ko Bo Ichi or Kogeki Bobi' is a complex tactic and strategy, the practice of which, will challenge your mind. *A complex practice or training that challenges the mind gives you a better mental and psychological preparation.*

In my view, 'Ko Bo Ichi' is created especially for those "life and death" situations, where the space and time are narrow and short. Certainly this is not the only tactic, but undoubtedly one of the most effective ones in the Japanese Martial Strategy.

It gives you the 'mental fortitude', and 'the strategic advantage' to survive. Being a martial artist does not mean you will win every life and death situation, it simply means that you are better prepared if you train hard.

Never forget the following:

"Technique over strength, tactics over aggression."

The scientific secret of 'Ko Bo Ichi' in martial strategy is hidden in:

The synchronization of *'Psychological'* training with the *'Physiological'* one.

Not only your 'Mind and Body' should become one, but also the 'Technique and Tactic' should properly merge with it. Therefore, 'Ko Bo Ichi' is more than just a unity of offense and defense, it is **'a strategic merger'.**

PAPER 6

NAGASHI ME: LET THE EYES ROLL

In the previous paper, I highlighted that in a 'life-threatening' situation, 'the psychology of survival' becomes relevant, and hence we need to have the synch of our 'Mind and Body' as quickly as possible in order to have a speedy reaction.

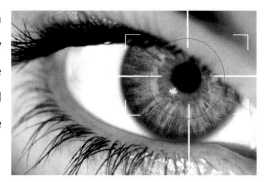

But can our body react quickly enough, if our eyes are not coordinated properly? Well, scientifically and in practice we can say no, it is not possible!

Since the eyes lead the body, and not the other way around, in order for our mind and body to react timely, we need to have a proper coordination of eyes with our head movement as well as with our entire body.

Regretfully, '*Nagashi Me* 流目' (Eye movement) is not well-emphasized in modern martial way or martial sport these days, but it plays a vital and strategic role in traditional martial arts.

By establishing a proper coordination of eyes and body movements, you can increase speed, and maximize efficiency in delivering techniques.

But before everything, let us first have a brief scientific introduction to types of 'Eye movements' and their functions.

TYPES OF EYE MOVEMENTS:

Conjugate eye movements are those that preserve the angular relationship between the right and left eyes. For example, when you move both eyes left and then right, a conjugate movement is made. Up and down movements and combinations of vertical and lateral movements also fall into the conjugate category.

Vergence eye movements are ones where the angle between the eyes changes. For example, hold your index finger in front of your nose. Now move your finger towards and away from your face, all the while fixating on your finger tip. As you move your finger closer to your face both eyes will converge and as you move your finger away from your face, your eyes will diverge.

Saccadic eye movements are very fast jumps from one eye position to another. To make a saccadic move, pick two objects at some distance from each other and look first at one then at the other. Because saccadic movements are so very fast, it may be difficult to see the eye movements as discrete jumps.

Smooth pursuit movements are just as their name implies. The eyes move smoothly instead of in jumps. They are called pursuit because this type of eye movement is made when the eyes follow an object. Therefore, to make a pursuit movement, look at your forefinger at arm's length and then move your arm left and right while fixating your finger tip."[33]

In Martial Strategies, 'Saccadic' and 'Smooth pursuit' eye movements are highly applicable and important. Practically, both can be done without moving your head. Why is this important?

Because, head is relatively heavy, 4.5 and 5 kg, which typically makes around **8%** of the body mass. Using eye movements without moving the head facilitates accuracy in tracking of high speed opponents. In combative situations, allowing your eyes move instead of your head, will prevent your body to become imbalanced, especially, when you are facing more than one opponent.

Vision is our most dominant sense. **20%** of the nerve fibers leaving the eyes go to our neck and inner ear (vestibular system)[34], which has more direct connection to our balance instead of visual cortex. When the body is off balanced, the brain requires that eyes take it under control. You can see this by spinning your friend on a chair and stop his rotation, then in his eyes you can see the saccadic movements that they are looking for a point of focus to maintain balance.

Our brain receives information from our eyes (eyes acting as lenses) and integrates it with other senses such as hearing, touch and movement; therefore, in combat, swinging your head unnecessarily to locate your opponent(s) or to track their movements will put your body at risk of being imbalanced and will reduce your speed.

Of course in martial strategies, allowing your eyes to naturally take information from the scene is the basic and fundamental step towards an advanced level of mental state, which is known as **'Kyo-Jitsu' 虚実**. *The understanding of 'Kyo-Jitsu' and its connection with 'Nagashi Me' will be a strategic advantage in martial arts.* But what is 'Kyo-Jitsu'?

KYO-JITSU:

It is a mental state and an application that has roots in teachings of 'Inyo' or 'Yin-Yang' and it literally means 'Emptiness or Fullness' / 'False or Truth'. While the kanji for **'Kyo 虚'** makes reference to words such as 'Emptiness, Hollow, False, Surprise, and Not ready'; the kanji for **'Jitsu 実'** directs us to meanings such as 'Fullness, Truth and Readiness'.

Here I briefly explain by asking this question: When is the best time to attack? When we can get the opponent off guard, right? But when our opponent is NOT READY?
Often our opponent is not ready when:
- Their concentration is taken away and broken;
- They are surprised with our unexpected moves;
- They are breathing in!

In all the above scenarios, there is an "emptiness" or a sort of absence. For example, why attacking when the opponent is breathing in? Because our opponent needs oxygen and he is out of air.

This is an example of 'Kyo' emptiness (when body is empty from Oxygen or it is with less energy), hence that's the best time to attack.

Contrary to 'Kyo', in 'Jitsu' our opponent is FULL of 'Ki' and energy. They have full concentration and awareness. When they are fully concentrated in our physical and mental movements, there is no opening; therefore, we had better not attack.

When your opponents are in the mind state of 'Jitsu', striking them may put you in danger. What will happen? Well, either you get stuck and are forced to counterattack or you won't get through at all. *Therefore, **the best strategy is, while maintaining your 'Jitsu', you should alter your opponent's state of mind from 'Jitsu' to 'Kyo'.***

Depending on what school and style, this can be done by proper footwork, body movements and if practicing weaponry, via weapon movements as well. But what happens when the state of 'Jitsu' changes to 'Kyo'?

Well, normally our opponent goes backward to maintain distance. They may become 'defensive' and strike hastily and hurriedly to your advantage or they may do nothing, simply because they are off guarded.

*The Author in guard with Naginata
(Japanese Classical Pole Weapon)*

Is there any strategy that would help to maintain our 'Jitsu'? Certainly, it is called '**Heijoshin** 平常心'. Literally this is a three part kanji that stands for: '***Hei** 平*' meaning 'steady'; '***Jo** 常*' meaning 'constant' and '***Shin** 心*' meaning mind or heart (the whole inner essence of an individual). Heijoshin can be translated as *"maintaining the state of mind at all times/in all situations"*.

Well, staying 'calm' in any circumstances seems logical, but it is not that easy to apply. In order to 'keep your mental state', you need to avoid four states of mind. These are often known as '***Shikai** 四戒*' (Four Prohibitions).

THE FOUR PROHIBITIONS:

In any circumstances, especially in combat, you should avoid the following mental states:

'***Kyo-Ku-Gi-Waku*** 恐怖疑惑'

- **Kyo:** Surprise
- **Ku:** Fear
- **Gi:** Doubt
- **Waku:** Confusion / Hesitation

What do human beings normally do when they are 'surprised'? In most cases, they hold their breath, have their eyes wide open, and don't move. In which case, the opponent will overpower them easier. Similarly, when humans are in 'fear', they feel they cannot move and their motions become slow.

Also if they 'doubt' the opponent's movements, they often become indecisive and slow in reactions. And of course when they are in the state of 'confusion', they get puzzled and hesitate to react.

Those four should be avoided in order to have 'Heijoshin' – the mental stability.

And here it comes, the connection between 'Nagashi Me' and 'Kyo-Jitsu':

Your eyes must carefully but naturally gather timely information on:

- When your opponent is breathing in, and is in 'Kyo' state of mind;
- How, when and to which direction your opponent moves;
- What are their weaponry movements;
- Are those moves '***Kyo-Jitsu Konko*** 虚実混交' a mix of truth and untruth, i.e. 'deceiving' or 'real'? ***While your eyes must scan your opponent's entire body and surroundings, they must not show any sign of 'fear', 'doubt', and 'confusion'.***

CONCLUSION:

If you think deeper about 'Kyo-Jitsu', underneath you may find a form of *'cause and effect'*. For instance, 'emptiness' causes 'activeness'. Like an open Kamae (guard) invites an attack. But is this open Kamae a lack of skill or a calculated risk to lure you to attack? Is your opponent's Kamae open due to his ignorance or is it purposefully left open?

Here is when you need to consider the following fact in martial strategies:
'It is not just important __what__ you see, it is important __how__ you see it.'

What you see might be just a mishmash of truth or untruth, reality or unreality and much of it could be just distractive and divertive. Therefore, it is highly important 'how' you see things.

Do not forget that your eyes are connected to your brain and your brain is shaping your mind and thoughts, and they both can influence your action and reaction. *What you see and perceive may change your state of mind from 'Kyo' to 'Jitsu or vice versa.* So, always take the following three steps, but in the shortest matter of time:

"Visualize, Analyze, Actualize."

For sure as you excel in your training, you will learn how to imagine yourself in place of your opponent and develop your skills to predict their moves. Once you are at that level, all you need to do is: *"Visualize the action, actualize the vision."* Therefore, in order to gain effective natural martial vision, **'let the eyes roll'**

PAPER 7

SHISHIN: LET THE MIND FLOW

In the previous paper I talked about the strategic importance of eye movements and their connection with the state of mind. In this paper I want to look deeper into how brain and mind can work better for a martial artist and what could be the best practice for having sharper brain and mind.

The Kanji for '**Shishin** 止心'stands for 'stopped mind', i.e. when your mind stands on one place. Some may confuse this with 'Mushin' (No Mind) of Zen Buddhism, but this is different. 'Shishin', is a state when your mind gets stuck. Like a detective, obsessed with a case, who tries to solve a crime mystery, but the more he concentrates the harder it gets to solve. 'Shishin' also finds its meaning when you pay too much attention to one issue, whilst ignoring the other ones.

The concept of 'Shishin' has roots in Taoism (Daoism), which encourages its followers to be in flow and harmony with the nature. Its philosophy has also greatly influenced the Japanese martial arts.

Lao-Tzu, the ancient Chinese philosopher and poet, best known as the author of the 'Tao Te Ching'[35] and the founder of philosophical 'Taoism', has a famous quote:

"Water is the softest thing, yet it can penetrate mountains and earth, this shows clearly, the principle of softness overcoming hardness". Similar quotes has been used by many martial art actors in various movies and interviews, encouraging martial art fans to be like "water". But the key factor here is that in that context, water is effective as long as it flows. No matter how effective water is, once it gets stuck in one place, it gets rotten.

'Shishin' also points out the same key factor. That is, in order for your mind to be effective, it should not get stuck in one place and it must move.

But let us explore this scientifically, by first studying the functions of 'Brain & Mind' in brief.

THE FUNCTION OF BRAIN:

In the world of **'neuroscience'**, one must answer many challenging questions about the brain. But the easiest and most fundamental questions are, 'why do we have a brain?' and 'What is it for?'

Some might answer: We have brains to think and to perceive the world.

Well, according to the Neuroscientist, Dr. Daniel Wolpert of University of Cambridge, that is completely wrong.

According to Dr. Wolpert, *"We have a brain for one reason, and one reason ONLY, and that is to produce adaptable and complex movements. Movement is the only way you have of affecting the world around you. Everything else goes through contraction of muscles. For example in communication, speech, gestures, writing, and sign language, they are all mediated through contractions of your muscles. So, it is really important to remember that sensory, memory, and cognitive processes are all important, BUT they are only important to either drive or suppress future movements"*. [36]

With this brief argument, we can subscribe that 'movement' is the most important function of the brain. Now let us quickly check out the function(s) of the mind.

THE FUNCTIONS OF MIND:

Mind has three distinctive functions: 'Thinking', 'Feeling', and 'Wanting'

- **Thinking** is to create meaning and to make sense of events. It sorts the events into named categories and continually tells us: 'what is happening', 'this is how to make sense and understand', and 'notice this or that'. This function of mind helps us to figure out things.

- **Feeling** is to assess, evaluate and monitor what is created by the thinking function. It evaluates how positive or negative the events are around us. It continually tells us: 'this is how we should feel about what is going on'; 'you are doing something good or something bad'.

- **Wanting** is to inject force or energy to action in maintaining what is desirable and possible. It continually tells us: 'this is what we should go for', 'this is worth going for', 'this doesn't worth going for', and 'hold on to it' or 'let it go'.

The three distinctive functions of mind can be displayed in the following table.

THINKING	FEELING	WANTING

- Analyzing - Comparing - Clarifying - Judging - Determining - Perceiving - Synthesizing....	- Calm - Worried - Excited - Anxious - Happy - Sad - Depressed - Stressed	- Motive - Goal - Purpose - Desire - Agenda - Value.....

There is a dynamic interrelation among 'thinking', 'feeling' and 'wanting'. Each is continually influencing the other two. For instance, when you are suddenly being attacked, you feel fear and you want to either defend yourself or flee the situation. Or if your child is forced to attend the training in the dojo, he will try to avoid going there, and if he complies, he will feel bored.

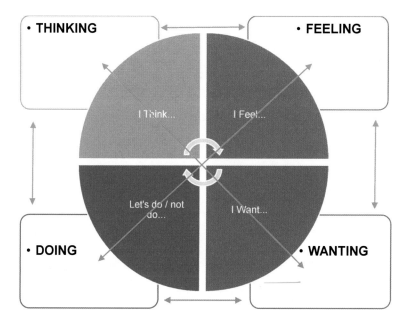

In a dynamic process, these three functions are constantly influencing each other and are intimately interacting. Now, knowing the functions of brain and mind, are they separate? Not at all! Brain and mind are totally related.

THE MIND AND BRAIN RELATIONS:

A. Straightforward causality – Brain causes mind. This relationship is disconcertingly unproblematic. It is very clear for neuroscience that brains are entirely capable of causing minds, and they do.

B. Direct correspondence – Mind is the same as brain activity. What occurs in brain, amongst other events, is minds. It seems at the moment that the kind of language we typically use to discuss mind will increasingly be replaced by which describes brain events – ultimately perhaps brain algorithms.

C. Neural correlation – Neural activity correlates with consciousness. When neural activity correlates with consciousness, its characteristic patterns generate mind. This means for every mind state there is also a brain state.[37]

Now that we are familiar with the functions of the brain and mind, and we are clear that they are related, here the question is:

How does 'Shishin – stopped mind' occur? What could cause the mind to stop in one place?

There could be two answers for this:

1. Perhaps due to the *overwhelming incompatibility*. While brain and mind are related, they are two different entities: **One is 'Physical', and the other 'Mental'.** The amazing complexity of brains persuades us to believe that minds are metaphysical when they are not. From neuroscience point of view, there is no way that a material thing – the brain, can relate to the mind – as a metaphysical thing.

Sadly, many young martial art practitioners in commercial training halls are often led to believe that there is something metaphysical going on in their brain and training, and with meditation and exercise, it will furnish them with a kind of super human strengths. Such misleading beliefs could cause the mind to struggle in duality.

2. Perhaps when you get caught in those 'loops', when you are thinking about one single event over and over again. Or when you are overthinking a decision.

Overthinking, is when you can't think about anything else. Imagine there is a physics problem and you can't solve it, you think about it over and over again with no luck. You decide to step out of it and take a break, next day some solutions come to your mind. Why? Because you let your mind move away and you stepped out of that loop.

These are very much relevant to the martial artists and their practices. Imagine at the moment that you see an opening guard in your opponent, instead of using the opportunity to attack, you keep contemplating on whether your attack must be with your right hand or your left one, or thinking overly on 'what ifs'. E.g. what will happen if your attack is missed, etc. Such prolonged contemplations may take the opportunities away from you to succeed.

Jujutsu - Throw

HOW TO HAVE A SHARPER MIND AND BRAIN IN MARTIAL ARTS:

I recommend martial artists to actively practice the followings:

1. **Form a martial art brain storming or interactive group. Attend martial arts seminars and lectures as often as possible.** According to Dr. Oscar Ybarra, associate psychology Professor at the University of Michigan: "*When you interact with other people, it is likely that structures in the frontal lobe that are responsible for 'executive functions'—like planning, decision making, and response control—get fired up.*" Regular discussion with your focus group about your martial techniques, their anatomy, history, culture, etc. will boost your mind and brain.

2. **Maximize your training and have it regular.** Dr. Thomas Crook, an Expert on cognitive development and memory disorders says: "*Cardiovascular activity pumps more oxygen-rich blood to the brain, which is like giving a car a shot of gasoline. With that blood comes nutrients such as glucose, which fuels every cell in the brain.*"[38] Regularity is just as important as intensity. A sort of bi-weekly training or once every now and then won't produce much. You need to dedicate time, make it a routine, and commit to it.

3. **Try to practice more challenging and complex Kata (forms), pair work drills (Futari Randori), and Bunkai (applications).** *"The brain, like all muscles and organs, is a tissue, and its function declines with underuse and age. Beginning in our late 20s, most of us will lose about 1 percent annually of the volume of the hippocampus, a key portion of the brain related to memory and certain types of learning. Exercise though seems to slow or reverse the brain's physical decay, much as it does with muscles."*[39] Therefore the more complex, the best. It makes you stay focused, sharp and attentive. By doing pair work, you stay at present and your mind wouldn't juggle around and fly elsewhere.

CONCLUSION:

What you think, you become; what you feel, you attract; and what you want, you achieve. ***Do not forget that in martial strategies, dominancy or victory is not just by muscles, it also requires brain and mental strengths.***

As mentioned earlier, brain causes mind, but you need to be fully in control of it. Sometimes the mind's functions of 'wanting' or 'feeling' may force you to give up or stop practicing. Sometimes your mind's function of 'thinking' gets clouded and your judgment becomes impaired, hence you might get distracted or derailed. *It is absolutely critical to realize that one way to stay in control of your mind is by doing proper martial arts training, where your mind and body can get the chance to synch and become one.*

Martial art activities *cause connections between neurons in the cerebellum*. Whilst such activities are hard physical training, they are also challenging for your brain and they will help your mind to develop. Genuine training in martial arts will assist you to stay in control of your mind and use your brain power for the purpose of good.

Mind is the greatest power, therefore, **'let the mind flow'**

PAPER 8

ITSUKU: LET THE BODY SWAY

In the previous paper I explained the concept of 'Shishin' (stopped mind), how mind and brain function and why the 'flow of mind' is crucial for martial artists. In this paper I am going to talk about another dangerous state that must be avoided by martial artists.

'**Itsuku** 居付く' is a state, when your body gets '**frozen**' and makes no reactions! And no movements. This often occurs when your mind is in the state of 'Shishin' and when you are shocked or taken by surprise.

Many instructors of martial arts believe that 'Itsuku' is just the result of not having 'the mind flow', but I personally believe that while the mind has a major role in causing the body to freeze, there are a few physical issues that could also cause the body to stagnate and not react timely.

To better understand 'Itsuku', let us first have a brief scientific analysis about our body movements.

HUMAN BODY MOMEMENTS:

Joints and their functions in body movements:

Human beings can walk and move their body because of their 'joints'. Joints connect two different parts of the body and enable body movements. The human body contains several bones joined together at different places.

Humans can bend or rotate their body parts only at joints. Each body part is capable of different movements; therefore, it is controlled by different types of joints. They include:

A. **Pivot** joints allow for rotation around an axis, such as between the first and second cervical vertebrae, which allows for side-to-side rotation of the head.

B. **Hinge** joint of the elbow works like a door hinge.

C. **Saddle** joint is the articulation between the trapezium carpal bone and the first metacarpal bone at the base of the thumb.

D. **Planar** (or Plane) joints, such as those between the tarsal bones of the foot, allow for limited gliding movements between bones.

E. **Condyloid** (or Ellipsoidal) joint is the radiocarpal joint of the wrist.

F. **Ball-and-socket** joints are the hip and shoulder joints. [40]

Please see the image in the next page and follow the joints functions.

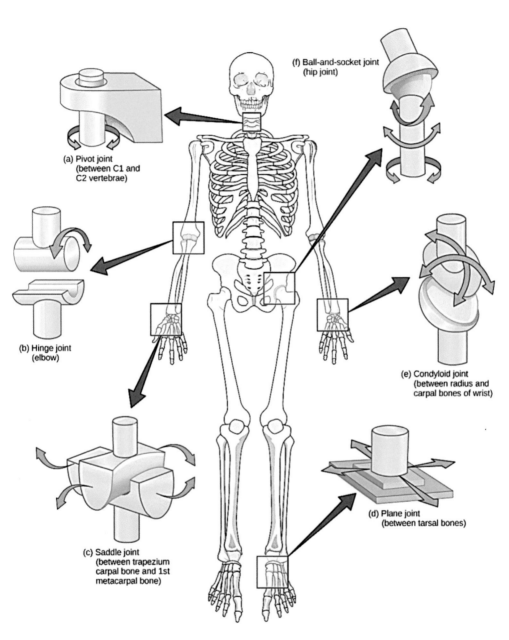

Types of Joints
Image by Boundless Biology

98

The functions of the joints can be described as followings:

Planar Joints: These joints allow for gliding movements; therefore, the joints are sometimes referred to as gliding joints. The range of motion is limited and does not involve rotation.

Hinge Joints: one bone moves while the other remains stationary, similar to the hinge of a door. The elbow is an example of a hinge joint. The knee is sometimes classified as a modified hinge joint.

Pivot Joints: This structure allows rotational movement, as the rounded bone moves around its own axis. An example of a pivot joint is the joint of the first and second vertebrae of the neck that allows the head to move back and forth. The joint of the wrist that allows the palm of the hand to be turned up and down is also a pivot joint.

Condyloid Joints: This is also sometimes called an ellipsoidal joint. This type of joint allows angular movement along two axes, as seen in the joints of the wrist and fingers, which can move both side to side and up and down.

Saddle Joints: They allow angular movements similar to Condyloid joints, but with a greater range of motion. An example of a saddle joint is the thumb joint, which can move back and forth and up and down; it can move more freely than the wrist or fingers.

Ball and Socket Joints: This organization allows the greatest range of motion, as all movement types are possible in all directions. Examples of ball-and-socket joints are the shoulder and hip joints. [41]

Muscles and their functions in body movements:

The muscular and tendons system is also responsible for the movement of the human body. We have over 640 muscles and basically they are categorized in three[42]:

A. **Skeletal Muscle** is the only voluntary muscle tissue in the human body that is controlled consciously. Every physical action that one consciously performs requires skeletal muscle. They are connected to the bones by tough, fibrous tissues called tendons. When one moves a muscle, the force of this movement passes from the muscle through its associated tendon. The tendon applies this force to initiate movement of the connected bone and associated joint. Muscles, bones and joints together make a process system called 'musculoskeletal'. Most of the muscles and tendons in this system have attachments to the bones in your arms, legs, chest, abdomen, face and neck.

B. Cardiac Muscle: Found only in the heart, cardiac muscle is responsible for pumping blood throughout the body. Cardiac muscle tissue cannot be controlled consciously, so it is an involuntary muscle. While hormones and signals from the brain adjust the rate of contraction, cardiac muscle stimulates itself to contract. The natural pacemaker of the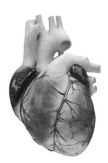
heart is made of cardiac muscle tissue that stimulates other cardiac muscle cells to contract. Because of its self-stimulation, cardiac muscle is considered to be auto rhythmic or intrinsically controlled.

C. Visceral Muscle is found inside of organs like the stomach, intestines, and blood vessels. The weakest of all muscle tissues, visceral muscle makes organs contract to move substances through the organ. Because visceral muscle is controlled by the unconscious part of the brain, it is known as involuntary muscle.

That is it cannot be directly controlled by the conscious mind. The term "smooth muscle" is often used to describe visceral muscle because it has a very smooth, uniform appearance when viewed under a microscope.

Now that we have got familiar with the basics of human body movements, let us take a few moments and think about the followings:

This is a fact that *in order for human body to move, it needs mind, and mind needs brain.* It is also a fact that 'Shishin' can cause 'Itsuku' (Stopped mind causes body to stop). However, since human body is such a complex system, it seems 'Shishin' cannot be the only factor for body to get frozen. Let us see the following factors.

HUMAN BODY IN STRESSFUL AND THREATENING SITUTIONS

Scientifically, what happens when one is in a threatening situation?

- The senses sharpen. Pupils dilate so one can see more clearly, even in darkness. Hairs stand on end, making them more sensitive to their environment, and muscles tighten, which will make them appear larger, hopefully intimidating the opponent.

- The cardio-vascular system leaps into action, with the heart pump rate going from one up to five gallons per minute and our arteries constricting to maximize pressure around the system whilst the veins open out to ease return of blood to the heart.

- The respiratory system joins in as the lungs, throat and nostrils open up and breathing speeds up to get more air in the system so the increased blood flow can be re-oxygenated. The blood carries oxygen to the muscles, allowing them to work harder. Deeper breathing also helps us to scream more loudly!

- Fat from fatty cells and glucose from the liver are metabolized to create instant energy.

- Blood vessels to the kidney and digestive system are constricted, effectively shutting down systems that are not essential. A part of this effect is reduction of saliva in the mouth. Sweat glands also open, providing an external cooling liquid to our over-worked system.

- Endorphins, which are the body's natural pain killers, are released. When one is fighting, one does not want to be bothered with pain that can be put off until later.

- The natural judgment system is also turned down and more primitive responses take over; this is a time for action rather than deep thought.[43]

So, while we can imagine that stress, anxiety, and threat can certainly affect one's mind, the 'physical changes' as outlined above can also influence human body to 'freeze' during perceiving a threat or a fight.

Hormones such as *endorphins, adrenaline and cortisol* have great impact in physical changes. As mentioned above, *in highly stressful situations and threats the natural judgment system is turned down and more primitive responses take over and muscles tighten, all of which have direct influence on our action/reaction time.*

Perhaps while the philosophy of Budo tries to address the state of 'Itsuku' based on the state of mind, we can respectively add that according to the science of body movements and on the basis of physical changes that occur during a fighting event, there are also physical factors that cause the body to freeze.

But for martial artists the topic does not end here. If we just put the 'Cardiac' and 'Visceral' muscles and their functions which are not controlled consciously aside, and just focus on the 'Skeletal Muscle', then we may even reach to a strategic operational point, and that is 'movements and coordination'.

MOVEMENTS AND COORDINATION:

Movements of your musculoskeletal system are typically under your conscious control. When you want to move your body, a portion of your brain called 'the motor cortex' sends an electrical signal to the appropriate muscle through your spinal cord and local nerves. This muscle contracts and initiates movement.

As they move, the muscle and its associated joint send feedback signals up through your nerves to a section of your brain called the cerebellum. Together, the outward and inward nerve signals passing between your brain and musculoskeletal system give you the ability to coordinate, and fine-tune your body's movements with position.

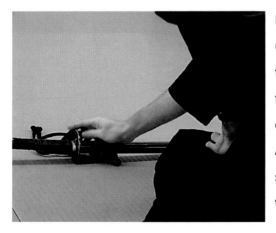

Even for a movement as simple as picking up your 'Sword', you can scarcely imagine trying to consciously specify the sequence, force, amplitude, and speed of the contractions of every muscle concerned. And yet, if we are healthy, we all make such movements all the time without even thinking of them.

The decision to pick up your 'Sword' is accompanied by increased electrical activity in the frontal region of the cortex. The neurons in the frontal cortex then send impulses down their axons to activate the motor cortex itself. Using the information supplied by the visual cortex, the motor cortex plans the ideal path for the hand to follow and reach the 'Sword'. The motor cortex then calls on other parts of the brain, such as the central grey nuclei and the cerebellum, which help to initiate and co-ordinate the activation of the muscles in sequence.

The axons of the neurons of the primary motor cortex descend all the way into the spinal cord, where they make the final relay of information to the motor neurons of the spinal cord. These neurons are connected directly to the muscles and cause them to contract. Finally, by contracting and pulling on the bones of the arm and hand, the muscles execute the movement that enables the 'Sword' to be picked up.

In addition, *to ensure that all of these movements are fast, precise, and coordinated, the nervous system must constantly receive sensory information from the outside world and use this information to adjust and correct the hand's trajectory.* [44]

The nervous system achieves these adjustments chiefly by means of the cerebellum, which receives information about the positions in space of the joints and the body from the proprioceptors.

Speaking of the motor cortex and task, here comes the most important practice for any martial artist, and that is "Muscle Memory".

MUSCLE MEMORY:

Of course muscle memory is not a memory stored in your muscles, but memories stored in your brain that are much like a cache of frequently enacted tasks for your muscles. *It is actually a motor learning of the brain, which forms procedural memory that involves consolidating a specific motor task into memory through repetition.*[45]

When a movement is repeated over time, a long-term muscle memory is created for that task, eventually allowing it to be performed without conscious effort. *This process decreases the need for attention and creates maximum efficiency within the motor and memory systems.*

During learning a motor task, at first movements are often slow, stiff and easily disrupted. But with constant practice, execution of motor task becomes smoother, faster and the limb and muscle stiffness get decreased, making the performance seem *without conscious effort.*

And perhaps this is a very strategic training for not falling into 'Shishin' and Itsuku' traps! If muscle memory gets practiced <u>with intent</u>, it will certainly strengthen both body and mind.

CONCLUSION:

To understand the science of body movements and human movement skills, you need to raise your awareness on both aspects of 'physical' and 'mental' states.

In broad sense, human movement is naturally rhythmic that we alternate and rest. Even breathing, speaking, and blinking among others have rhythm and dynamics, but some have more inconsistence and unpredictable patterns.

As in martial arts, 'Body', 'Action', 'Space', 'Time', and 'Energy' are visible experiences, you need to pay attention to what you project to your opponent. Your body and its action occupies space, takes time and burns energy; therefore, **in the science of body movement, the martial strategy is *to how effectively and efficiently reduce the amount of 'space', 'time' and 'energy' while facing your opponent. Any physical deficiency and miscalculation in 'space', 'time' and 'energy' might result in your body movement to fail and get frozen.***

Since your body, action, space, time, and energy are controlled, assessed and defined by your brain and mind, you need to have both mental and physical 'discipline' to succeed, and for that, exercising *'muscle memory'* with proper intent, and when applicable with passive resistance are of absolute necessity.

'Itsuku' is a dangerous trap to fall into; therefore, in order to avoid, **'let the body sway'**

SWAN SONG

In conclusion, martial arts in Japan are deeply rooted in their culture and history. I recall *'Emperor'* an American-Japanese post-World War II movie of 2012 directed by Peter Webber, in which a remarkable cultural fact was stated.

*"If you understand **'Devotion'**, you understand Japan. There are two words one should know: **'Tatemae** 建前' (the way things appear), and **'Honne** 本音' (the way things really are). When you look at Japan, you see the most modern and Westernized of Asian countries, but that is 'Tatemae', the surface. 'Honne' is the true heartbeat of Japan, which is 2000 years old and has nothing to do with the West. Japan runs on the ancient Warrior code of 'loyalty' and 'obedience' ".[46]*

Although the notion of 'Tatemae and Honne' may be synonymous to the common concept of 'public' and 'private' display, which of course could be found in every culture, this contrast of one's true feelings and desire, as opposed to what is displayed in public is a supreme importance in *'managing conflict'* in the Japanese culture. The conceptual culture of 'Tatemae and Honne' can also be found in

Tibor Herczeg, Renshi - performing a Kojido Todi-Jutsu Kata - 'Hakutsuru'- The White Crane

the Japanese martial arts. For example, in Bunkai (applications) there is:

'Omote 面' (what it seems), **'Ura** 裏' (what it means), and **'Honto** 本当' (what it really is) i.e. the hidden truth, which is not vivid. Sun Tzu, in 'The Art of War' writes:

"All men can see these tactics whereby I conquer, but what <u>none can see</u> is the <u>'strategy'</u> out of which victory is evolved."[47]

With view to Tzu's writing, from experience I can say, *while it is not that difficult to learn a technique and it is not that difficult to realize a tactic, it is certainly hard to understand, and much harder to create strategy.*

Keep in mind that: '**strategies are <u>hidden</u> beneath the tactics.**'

Therefore, for better understanding of what you do as martial arts, you are recommended to go deeper for the knowledge. No matter if you do Japanese - Okinawan martial arts for fitness, self-defense, or for keeping traditions, it is highly important to remember that: **Many died to learn what you have been taught.**

For several centuries, countless of Warriors lost their lives and got injured until their techniques and tactics got refined to pass on; therefore, *please do not take martial arts light.*

It is almost forty years now that I am practicing various martial arts and at some point during my childhood and youth, I did martial sport at national and international levels. While I am proud of my past athletic achievements, as I grew older and more mature, I learnt that there is much more into martial arts and I realized that sadly martial sport as we see today, especially with view to the teaching of Kata and self-defense cannot even scratch the surface of what lays beneath. Therefore, I have decided to devote myself to facilitate Bujutsu and to promote the essence of martial traditions, strategies and the understanding of what is '**Hidden**'.

The Author, embracing his Katana

Learn to act like a Swan,
calm on surface...
paddle beneath with purpose;

Learn to act like a Swan,
ballet with enemy...
meet the foe readily;

Learn to act like a Swan,
protect with honor...
never deep in slumber;

Learn to act like a Swan,
gentle with patience...
humble and gracious.

Mosi Dorbayani

APPENDIX:

FUNCTIONALITY: A NOTE ON SELF-DEFENSE

If you want to practice Japanese-Okinawan martial arts with the goal to learn self-defense, I suggest you first find answers to these questions: What is the self that I am defending? What is my true goal? Do I want to protect my house, car or belongings, or do I want to be able to defend my life in a rough neighborhood? Or do I need it to build up self-confidence just in case I might need it one day? Once you identified your goal(s), then you need to take up a functional system or school that can assist you best. You might even consider attending different systems and schools to achieve your goals.

A perfect, know it all school hardly exists!

For example, some schools or systems may not teach any functional techniques that might be practical in confined places like inside a car, small storage rooms, tight corridors or in a crowded area like packed buses or undergrounds. Therefore, you might need to objectively consider different schools and systems for different purposes and certainly without 'style prejudice'.

You also need to remember that the true process of acquiring self-defense with empty hands is demanding and is not a quick fix as often portrayed on TV or YouTube. It requires commitment and dedication to practice. Of course in order to protect one's body or belongings there are far more easier ways and affordable equipment and technology available, even one can simply get a dog to escort them, why bother going through years of painful physical and mental training. So, it seems that it is not all about protecting material things, but perhaps more about principles.

Speaking of principles, ideally everyone is expected to live by a set of principles for the purpose of good, and in order to maintain that, one should not only build up a positive character to support it, but also physically and mentally be strong enough to stand for it and protect it. *Our 'Values', 'Principles' and 'Rights' as human beings are among elements that define us for who we are, the true self, and the one worth defending.*

There are always ways to succeed in a fight without actually fighting, BUT when absolutely as the last resort you have to apply your martial skills to protect your rights and life, then you need to have the practical and functional skills.

There are some deluded instructors out there around the world including inside Japan with much distorted views of 'theoretical violence and confrontation'. Such views and techniques all may look 'impressive and neat' in the dojo, but they do not work in reality!

If every move is instructed and you always know what is coming, then how are you supposed to react and survive in a real life situation where often actions are unpredictable, unexpected and not defined by rules?

I am often asked: "Are the modern martial way (Gendai Budo) styles or even Mixed Martial Arts (MMA full- contact combat sport) practical and functional for self-defense? Well, learners need to objectively investigate for themselves and benchmark the school's curriculum against their objectives. Some schools do not teach self-defense at all. They stick to their set of drills, physical training and / or sparring which may resemble techniques for self-defense, albeit a sort of pseudo combat activity, if you will.

The fact of the matter is that throughout history martial arts have got so heavily influenced by religious doctrines and political agendas. And although they were originally created for battles, combats and civil self-protection, today they are mostly practiced as martial way (Budo) for *'self-perfection'*, fitness or recreation. Therefore, for the sake of safety for mass practices, they have to follow certain rules.

Honestly, it will be highly improbable to be able to apply martial sport techniques or regulated practices in a notorious street or a rough neighborhood. In the real combat there is no rule, the street is not furnished by tatami, the parameter of the fight outbreak is not limited to the space of a metal cage, it is not limited in time or rounds, and has no luxury of weight category, wrapping hands, gloves or any sort of protection.

I know that there are some training centers out there, where they teach illegal measures and techniques which are completely unjustified, unethical and immoral; therefore, you had better be watchful and pick your martial style and school sensibly. And remember, **'YouTube' is not your Sensei!**

'Nagamine Shoshin Sensei' once said: *"The Western world is not the only place where charlatan Karate teachers exist. We too, right here in Okinawa and Japan, have our own fair share."* [48]

I remember watching a documentary video from late 'Anichi Miyagi Sensei', who said *"The world do not understand the language of martial arts"*.

Sadly the understanding of martial arts' language and culture is often limited to either martial sport, i.e. scoring points or just learning how to break boards, punch, kick, block, throw or cut. But let me assure you that this is not limited to the West and the Westerners. I did witness the same poor level of understanding and interpretation from a few Japanese instructors, even on the Japanese national TV.

Albeit, this misunderstanding is not just because of being ignorant or shallow. For example Japanese-Okinawan instructors often do not speak fluent English or any other international languages; therefore, to understand and being understood are often a challenge, especially about the details at advanced levels and strategies.

Regretfully students who also visit Japan or Okinawa often do not familiarize themselves with the Japanese language and its unique culture, which again adds up to the same level of misunderstanding. Even with having interpretation services, many things potentially get lost in translation especially if the interpreter is not a martial artist.

Another reason for the absence of full understanding is the lack of 'trust'. Many non-Japanese have traveled to Japan and managed to get representation appointments for their home countries. Whilst this may have only served as a photo op and a certificate for public display in order to justify their right to sell Kyu and Dan degrees, and most likely with no intention of genuinely continuing their learning with that master after all. Such experiences have made many instructors feel skeptical and not to easily open up to discuss details with their visiting students unless it is proven otherwise.

Or some go there to a relaxed dojo only to obtain a Dan Diploma from Japan to credit their proficiency and once it is received, they are done. They never even return to the same dojo/association. Seeing or hearing of such cases could also be a cause for Japanese-Okinawan instructors not to fully explain and disclose their knowledge unless the trust is established over time, hence another reason for limited understanding and knowledge.

And of course there are some who are just martial arts tourists; and as a result, what they learn and take away from a dojo, however still valuable, is certainly limited to their intention and time spent.

Nevertheless, very few centers are paying proper attention to the depth of martial culture and its 'hidden' teachings and strategies. And very few instructors really invest time to travel, study and research. Please think about it, if it was all about punching and kicking, or throwing and cutting, then most gangs from Harlem to Hanover would have been black belts and blade masters.

Of course in order to build up your body and to gain some confidence, learning any form of martial way or martial sport might be helpful, but certainly it is not the only way! American Football, Rugby, and Hockey among a few others can do the same and turn you to a strong, highly-spirited, go-get-it person. But if you want to strengthen your three aspects of 'Mind', 'Body' and 'Spirit' equally, try to improve your martial skills and above all learn them tactically and strategically, and then you need to make sure your choice of martial school and style serves your personal goals well.

While many schools in and outside Japan emphasize on 'Self-Perfection', some emphasize on the actual martial skills for 'Self-Protection'.

Exercising the true Japanese martial arts for self-defense is demanding. It is rarely understood and seldom taught by non-Japanese/Okinawan teachers; therefore, try to select your school and teacher carefully.

This does not mean if an instructor is Japanese then automatically what they teach is genuine and practical, nor does it mean that non-Japanese instructors are fraudulent. There are many non-Japanese instructors and schools that are stellar in their arts and system.

Many practitioners are often led to believe that it is impossible to truly master the Japanese martial arts unless you are Japanese or an apprentice living with a Japanese/Okinawan master. But such ideas are just propaganda in order to maintain dominancy over martial traditions, which have been feared to be taken over by other nationalities. However secret techniques are seldom taught and not to very many, if you are persistent, patient, honest and genuine in pursuing the art, most likely you will be privy to them.

On that note, *if available, try to learn at schools and centers where they are genuinely linked to the real source, preferably directly to the founder and to the main line of the school or organization.* Do your due diligence, watch their training sessions more than a couple of times, make proper inquiries, talk to experienced people, consult and gather information and finally make an informed decision.

There are students out there who call their masters 'Legendary' or a 'Living Legend'! In Japan and I believe in many other countries especially when a master is still alive, this may have a reverse interpretation, i.e. their students are trying to make a sale.

Many legends are simply not true, and many instructors are overly mystified and their abilities and teaching methods exaggerated. Try to avoid joining commercially oriented or so-called "McDojos", especially if you want to pursue self-defense and/or Japanese traditional martial arts.

Keep in mind that 'Technique' is a product of body and 'Tactic' is the production of a coordinated mind and body; therefore, training with intent is crucial.

While in reality of combat there is no guarantee for any application to succeed for 100%, there are certain styles/systems and centers, where you can learn genuine martial arts for self-defense to prepare you physically, mentally, and spiritually to face actual combat in a well-supervised, controlled and ethical environment.

Normally, such centers first familiarize you with the fundamentals of attack and counter scenarios and increase your level of confidence. Once your level of confidence is established at the proper level, then gradually they increase the intensity of your practice encountering passive and aggressive resistance, enforced and intensified by unexpected chaotic situations as closely to the actual conditions and intensity of a reality-based violent encounter.

Of course such training normally will not end there, they often teach you the applications of Kata (forms), which was traditionally meant for self-defense and they can scientifically guide you to learn more about your body movements, postures, its anatomy, and its good and bad habits, all for you to build up a martial body better prepared for real combat.

Furthermore, in pursue of self-defense, do not overlook the art of weaponry.
Studying the weaponry systems of martial arts is an integral, yet crucial part of learning self-defense.

THE IMPORTANCE OF LEARNING MARTIAL WEAPONS

Humans are "hunting" animals or creatures. They can manipulate objects to use them as weapons. The recorded history of mankind proves that humans have been using weapons for both hunting and self-defense and this nature is still vivid in the 21st century when people use fire arms for hunting or carry weapons for protection or law enforcement.

I often get this question: which one was created first, the unarmed or armed martial arts? With view to the history and the studies of Anthropology and Paleoanthropology, *there is no doubt that human being used bare hands ONLY when no weapon or other options were available to him.* Therefore, it is quite certain that the martial arts of weaponry had been around much earlier than the unarmed ones.

The Martial Arts of Weaponry in Japan and Okinawa:

Often there is a confusion about the Japanese and Okinawan martial arts of weaponry; therefore, for the sake of clarity, let us first get the terminologies and some basic concepts out of the way, then reason why learning martial weapons is important.

In Japanese, '***Kobudo*** 古武道' (Old Martial Way) and '***Koryu*** 古流' (Old / Traditional School) are normally considered synonymous, BUT there are a few distinctions between 'Kobudo' and 'Koryu', such as their origin, date, and the differences between their objective priorities on combat, morals, discipline and aesthetic forms.[49]

While 'Koryu' system is referred to schools and traditions prior to the Meiji Restoration in 1868, and can even be traced back to Nara Period in the 8th century, 'Kobudo' marks the beginning of the 'Tokugawa' period (1603-1868) also known as the 'Edo' period, when the total power was consolidated by the ruling 'Tokugawa clan'.[50]

'Kobudo' must not be confused with '**Okinawan Kobudo** 沖縄古武道', the weaponry system of Okinawan Martial Way or '**Ryukyu Kobujutsu** 琉球古武術 ', the weaponry system of Ryukyu Martial Skills/Arts.

'Okinawa/Okinawan Kobudo' and 'Ryukyu Kobujutsu' each cover different concepts, and they represent strictly the weapon practices of the Okinawa group of Islands. 'Okinawa Kobudo' is a term used by 'Matayoshi Shimpo Sensei' to describe his own system, while 'Ryukyu Kobujutsu' represents the system created by 'Taira Shinken Sensei'.

Some believe the first recorded history of using weaponry in Ryukyu (Okinawa) was about seven hundred years ago, when similar Okinawan weapons were used in a 100-year war, during which the islands were divided among three rival chiefs. The golden age of Ryukyu Kobujutsu was from the 17th to 19th centuries, producing great masters such as Soeishi, Sakugawa and Chatanyara.[51]

Okinawa Kobudo / Ryukyu Kobujutsu refers to the classical weapons most notably:

'**Rokushaku Bo** 棒' (Kun in Okinawan – a six foot Staff)

'**Sai** 釵' (Unsharpened fork like baton-dagger)

'**Tonfa** トンファー' (Handled club),

'**Kama** 鎌 / かま' (Sickle)

'**Nunchaku** ヌンチャク' (Two Sticks joint by chain or rope)

'**Tekko** 鉄甲' (Knuckle Dusters)

'**Tinbe-Rochin** 短い槍 - 盾 [JPN Lang.]' (Shield and Short Spear)

'**Eku** エーク/櫂' (Boat Oar of traditional Okinawan design) among others.

It is the common belief that weapons are traced back to the fishing and farming traditions and trades.

Okinawa Kobudo / Ryukyu Kobujutsu traditions were shaped by native Okinawan which arose within 'Aji', or the noble class, as well as borrowed methods from China, Taiwan, India, and a few other South East Asian countries that the Ryukyu Kingdom was trading with.

Okinawa Kobudo and Ryukyu Kobujutsu are taught by some forerunners of Karate; therefore, it is not unusual to see an occasional kick or empty-hand technique in a weaponry form (Kata). Inside Okinawa, Karate and Okinawa Kobudo/Kobujutsu are inseparable and both are the two wheels of the same cart, hence one can often see the practice of weaponry in Okinawan Karate curriculum or vice versa.

While Okinawan martial arts of weaponry was predominantly created for *'civil self-protection'* and influenced by the locals' lifestyles, the Japanese martial arts of weaponry was developed for the *'battlefields'*, mostly by the military might of the mainland Japan and Samurai, hence a huge difference in the execution of techniques, tactics, forms, and types of weapons.

'However Okinawan martial weapons and their methods are traditional, the Japanese martial weapons are professional and mostly military'.

Among popular Japanese weapons used by Samurai we can name:

'*Katana* 刀 / 日本刀' (Sword / Japanese Sword)

'*Naginata* なぎなた, 薙刀'(Pole weapon / Japanese Blade used by foot soldiers class, also popular with women warriors)

'*Yari* 槍' (A form of Spear)

'*Bo* 棒'(Long Staff)

'*Jo* 杖'(Short Staff)

'*Yumi* 弓'(Japanese Bows [Daikyu (大弓), long bow or Hankyu (半弓), shorter])

'**Koryu Bujutsu** 古流武術' Old School / Traditional Martial Skills of Japan also falls into two major forms of armed and unarmed combat, both complementing each other. There are many Koryu dojo and schools of martial strategies in Japan, some even as old as 600 years. Many Koryu centers in Japan are offering a wide range of curriculum. Such schools are often categorized as '**Sogo Bujutsu** 総合武術' offering 'comprehensive' martial skills development in both aspects of weaponry and unarmed martial strategies.

Among Japanese weaponry arts, we can highlight '**Kenjutsu** 剣術', the art of 'Swordsmanship', '**Iaijutsu** 居合術**'** the combative quick-draw sword technique, and as for close combat - often unarmed, we can name '**Jujutsu** 柔術' the 'Gentle Skills' of grappling among most popular forms of Koryu Bujutsu.

And of course there are plenty of schools and centers, where they put emphasis on character building and self-perfection, and mentor '**Iaido** 居合道', the 'Way of Sword Drawing' or '**Judo** 柔道', 'the 'Gentle Way'.

I am often asked this question:

"What is the difference between 'Kenjutsu' and 'Iaido'?" *Well, while 'Kenjutsu' is created and developed by warriors who actually experienced battlefields, 'Iaido' is often made by non-warriors and for the sake of self-perfection and sport.* And here it comes the underlining difference between 'Kobudo' and Koryu': In Kobudo / Budo the emphasis and priority is on "morality" before technique or skill, while in Koryu / Bujutsu, the emphasis and priority is given to "technique, skills, science or the actual art". While generally one joins Budo for spiritual-self-perfection, the followers of Bujutsu strive for the actual art, techniques and skills for <u>survival.</u>

Now, why learning martial weaponry is important?

There could be many reasons but here I will rest to outline a few:

1. However it is simply true that we do not live in Feudal Japan and warring state, and nobody can wear a Samurai Katana in public or carry a pair of Tonfa around, learning weaponry is a great way to preserve and pass on the ancient traditions.

2. In order to discover the new, one needs to understand the old.

3. There are very many useful 'hidden' lessons in the old arts of weaponry, some may very well serve you to understand the unarmed martial arts complexity better.

4. We do not necessarily learn weapons to use them, but by learning the arts of weaponry, we will understand its logic and how to defend ourselves against them. ***Studying the strategies, tactics and techniques of weaponry will assist us to understand how to react, counter and defend ourselves even with empty hands.*** That is the very reason why I highly recommend those interested in pursuing 'self-defense' to also study the art of weaponry.

Author with Okinawan Weapon - Tonfa

ADDENDUMS BY THE PUBLISHER

Hereafter, you are shared with some additional readings, which we found related to the author's articles in this publication. However some of the following literatures are available and accessible as public domain, we re-introduce them here with a few inputs from the author.

MARTIAL ARTS AND CULTURE

"If you take the culture away from the martial arts, then what you end up with, is nothing but violence." Mosi Dorbayani, Dojo Martial Magazine - Issue 106 - 2009

Bun Bu Ryo Do

The first kanji character '文 bun' literally means 'letter or writing'. In this context it means 'arts and science' or 'liberal arts' including the Japanese arts of Shodo (brush writing), Kado (flower arrangement) and Sado (tea ceremony).

In other words, it represents the mastery of the general education and the cultural studies. The second kanji character '武 Bu' means military. In this context it means military affairs or martial arts. The third kanji character '両 ryo' means both or as one. And the last kanji character, '道 do' means road or path.

This term is as old as the famous literary Heike Story of the 13th century. It is unknown when exactly this term was invented but the combination of two kanjis of 文 and 武 was popular in ancient Japan. Also this combination was used for the 42nd emperor, '**Monmu** 文武天皇' (683-707) in the 7th century.

Although the pronunciation of those kanjis were "Monmu" at the time, the meaning remained the same and it translates to: this emperor was to excel in both higher education and military affairs.[52] It emphasizes that the study of science and liberal arts is as important as the physical training, and both should be complementing each other.

'The Way of literary (pen) and the way of military (sword) as one'.

WARRIORS' CODE OF CONDUCT: MORALITY AND HUMANITY

"...every war has casualties, but in the study of Japanese martial strategy, one should remember that Bushido had never been about killing, but the 'cause' worth dying for." Mosi Dorbayani, at Budo Gala - Copenhagen, 2001.

Media and popular productions often misrepresented Japanese martial arts and their way of warriors. For example, in the late 1970s a documentary by 'Joy Pack Film' was made in title of *'Budo: The Art of Killing'*. While producers at very best had the promotion of Japanese martial arts at heart, the title and some narrations certainly mislead the public's perceptions about the Japanese martial arts and above all about the concepts of 'Bushido' and 'Budo'.

Arthur May Knapp, Historian, in his book 'In Feudal and Modern Japan', (Vol.1 - 1896), wrote: *"The Samurai of thirty years ago had behind him a thousand years of training in the*

Bushido: Way of the Warrior / Military knight Way

law of honor, obedience, duty, and self-sacrifice.... It was not needed to create or establish them. As a child he had but to be instructed, as indeed he was from his earliest years, in the etiquette of self-immolation"[53]

Brett and Kate McKay in their site 'The Art of Manliness' quoted: "Just a few decades after Japan's warrior class was abolished, U.S. President Teddy Roosevelt raved about a newly released book entitled *'Bushido: The Soul of Japan' (1899)*. He bought several dozen copies for family and friends." But what was the interpretation of Bushido in that book? 'Nitobe Inazo' Philosopher, Educator and Author, described the Samurai code of behavior: how warriors act in their personal and professional lives.

Dr. Nitobe Inazo (1862 - 1933)

Nitobe started writing that book in order to let the world know how Japanese people learn *'morals or ethics'* <u>without relying on the education of religion</u>. *He found that "Bushido" is essentially building Japanese moral obligation and ethical thinking.*

What readers may find awakening about Bushido is the emphasis on compassion, benevolence, and the other non-martial qualities that Nitobe describes. In short, here are Bushido's Eight Virtues as described by Nitobe:

1. Rectitude or Justice:

The most cogent precept in the code of the Samurai. Nothing is more loathsome to him than underhand dealings and crooked undertakings. The conception of Rectitude may be erroneous—it may be narrow. A well-known Bushi defines it as a power of resolution. Bushido refers not only to martial rectitude, but to personal rectitude: Rectitude or Justice is the strongest virtue of Bushido. A well-known samurai defines it this way: 'Rectitude is one's power to decide upon a course of conduct in accordance with reason, without wavering; to die when to die is right, to strike when to strike is right.' Another speaks of it in the following terms: 'Rectitude is the bone that gives firmness and stature. Without bones the head cannot rest on top of the spine, nor hands move or feet stand.

So 'without Rectitude neither talent nor learning can make the human frame into a Samurai.'

2. Courage:

Courage was scarcely deemed worthy to be counted among virtues, unless it was exercised in the cause of Righteousness. Bushido distinguishes between bravery and courage: Courage is worthy of being counted among virtues only if it's exercised in the cause of Righteousness and Rectitude. In his Analects, Confucius says: "Perceiving what is right and doing it not reveals a lack of Courage." Put this epigram into a positive statement, and it runs, "Courage is doing what is right." To run all kinds of hazards, to jeopardize one's self, to rush into the jaws of death—these are too often identified with Valor, and in the profession of arms such rashness of conduct—what Shakespeare calls, "valor misbegotten"—is unjustly applauded; but not so in the Precepts of Knighthood. Death for a cause unworthy of dying for, was called a "dog's death." "To rush into the thick of battle and to be slain in it," says a Prince of Mito, "is easy enough, and the merest churl is equal to the task; but," he continues, "it is true courage to live when it is right to live, and to die only when it is right to die," and yet the Prince had not even heard of the name of Plato, who defines courage as "the knowledge of things that a man should fear and that he should not fear." A distinction which is made in the West between moral and physical courage has long been recognized among Japanese.

In short, 'Courage is doing what is right.'

3. Benevolence or Mercy:

Love, magnanimity, affection for others, sympathy and pity, which were ever recognized to be supreme virtues, the highest of all the attributes of the human soul. Benevolence was deemed a princely virtue in a twofold sense;—princely among the manifold attributes of a noble spirit; princely as particularly befitting a princely profession.

Fortunately Mercy was not so rare as it was beautiful, for it is universally true that *"The bravest are the most tender, the loving are the daring."*

'*Bushi no nasaké*'—the tenderness of a warrior—had a sound which appealed at once to whatever was noble in them; not that the mercy of a Samurai was generically different from the mercy of any other being, but because it implied mercy where mercy was not a blind impulse, but where it recognized due regard to justice, and where mercy did not remain merely a certain state of mind, but where it was backed with power to save or kill.

As economists speak of demand as being effectual or ineffectual, similarly we may call the mercy of 'Bushi' effectual, since it implied the power of acting for the good or detriment of the recipient. Both Confucius and Mencius often said "*the highest requirement of a ruler of men is Benevolence*".

4. Politeness or Respect:

Politeness will be a great acquisition, if it does no more than impart grace to manners; but its function does not stop here. For propriety, springing as it does from motives of benevolence and modesty, and actuated by tender feelings toward the sensibilities of others, is ever a graceful expression of sympathy.

Its requirement is that we should weep with those that weep and rejoice with those that rejoice. Discerning the difference between obsequiousness and politeness can be difficult for casual visitors to Japan, but for a true man, courtesy is rooted in benevolence: courtesy and good manners have been noticed by every foreign tourist as distinctive Japanese traits. But Politeness should be the expression of a benevolent regard for the feelings of others; it's a poor virtue if it's motivated only by a fear of offending good taste.

'In its highest form, Politeness approaches love.'

5. Veracity or Truthfulness:

Lying or equivocation were deemed equally cowardly. The 'Bushi' held that his high social position demanded a loftier standard of veracity than that of the tradesman and peasant. *'Bushi no ichi-gon'*—the word of a samurai —was sufficient guaranty of the truthfulness of an assertion. His word carried such weight with it that promises were generally made and fulfilled without a written pledge, which would have been deemed quite beneath his dignity.

The regard for veracity was so high that, unlike the generality of Christians who persistently violate the plain commands of the Teacher not to swear, the best of samurai looked upon an oath as derogatory to their honor.

They did swear by different deities or upon their swords; but never has swearing degenerated into wanton form and irreverent interjection. To emphasize the words a practice of literally sealing with blood was sometimes resorted too.

From profession point of view, of all the great occupations of life, none was farther removed from the profession of arms than commerce. The merchant was placed lowest in the category of vocations,—the knight, the tiller of the soil, the mechanic, the merchant. The samurai derived his income from land and could even indulge, if he had a mind to, in amateur farming; but the counter and abacus were abhorred.

Commerce, therefore, in feudal Japan did not reach that degree of development which it would have attained under freer conditions. The obloquy attached to the calling naturally brought within its pale such as cared little for social repute.

Those who are well acquainted with Japanese history will remember that only a few years after the treaty ports were opened to foreign trade, feudalism was abolished, and when with it the Samurai's fiefs were taken and bonds issued to them in compensation, they were given liberty to invest them in mercantile transactions. Now one may ask, "Why could they not bring their much boasted veracity into their new business relations and so reform the old abuses?" Those who had eyes to see could not weep enough, those who had hearts to feel could not sympathize enough, with the fate of many a noble and honest samurai who signally and irrevocably failed in his new and unfamiliar field of trade and industry, through sheer lack of shrewdness in coping with his artful plebeian rival.

The ways of wealth, were not the way of honor. True Samurai, disdained money, believing that 'men must grudge money, for riches hinder wisdom.' Thus children of high-ranking Samurai were raised to believe that talking about money showed poor taste, and that ignorance of the value of different coins showed good breeding: 'Bushido' encouraged thrift, not for economic reasons so much as for the exercise of abstinence.

Luxury was thought the greatest menace to manhood, and severe simplicity was required of the warrior class. Accordingly counting and book keeping were done by low ranks or Priests.

If Bushido rejects a doctrine of quid pro quo rewards, the shrewder tradesman will readily accept it.

"Often have I wondered whether the Veracity of Bushido had any motive higher than courage. In the absence of any positive commandment against bearing false witness, lying was not condemned as sin, but simply denounced as weakness, and, as such, highly dishonorable."[54]

6. Honor:

The sense of honor, implying a vivid consciousness of personal dignity and worth, could not fail to characterize the samurai, born and bred to value the duties and privileges of their profession. Though the word ordinarily given now-a-days as the translation of Honor was not used freely, yet the idea was conveyed by such terms as *'Na'* (name) *'Men-moku'* (countenance), *'Guai-bun'* (outside hearing), reminding us respectively of the biblical use of "name," of the evolution of the term "personality" from the Greek mask, and of "fame." A good name—one's reputation, the immortal part of one's self, what remains being bestial—assumed as a matter of course, any infringement upon its integrity was felt as shame, and the sense of *'Ren-Chi-shin'* (shame) was one of the earliest to be cherished in juvenile education. "You will be laughed at," "It will disgrace you," "Are you not ashamed?" were the last appeal to correct behavior on the part of a youthful delinquent. Such a recourse to his honor touched the most sensitive spot in the child's heart, as though it had been nursed on honor while it was in its mother's womb; for most truly is honor a prenatal influence, being closely bound up with strong family consciousness.

Though Bushido deals with the profession of soldiering, it is equally concerned with non-martial behavior: The sense of Honor, a vivid consciousness of personal dignity and worth, characterized the Samurai. He was born and bred to value the duties and privileges of his profession. Fear of disgrace hung like a sword over the head of every Samurai … To take offense at slight provocation was ridiculed as *'short-tempered.'* As the popular adage put it: *'True patience means bearing the unbearable.'*

7. Loyalty:

Which was the key-stone making feudal virtues a symmetrical arch. Other virtues feudal morality shares in common with other systems of ethics, with other classes of people, but this virtue—homage and fealty to a superior—is its distinctive feature. Of course personal fidelity is a moral adhesion existing among all sorts and conditions of men,—a gang of pickpockets owe allegiance to a Fagin; but it is only in the code of chivalrous honor that 'Loyalty' assumes paramount importance. Loyalty as Japanese conceive it may find few admirers elsewhere, not because its conception is wrong, but because it is, forgotten, and also because we carry it to a degree not reached in any other country.

Economic reality has dealt a blow to organizational loyalty around the world. Nonetheless, true men remain loyal to those to whom they are indebted: Loyalty to a superior was the most distinctive virtue of the feudal era.

Since 'Bushido', like 'Aristotle' and some modern sociologists, conceived the state as antedating the individual—the latter being born into the former as part and parcel thereof—he must live and die for it or for the incumbent of its legitimate authority. Readers of 'Crito' will remember the argument with which 'Socrates' represents the laws of the city as pleading with him on the subject of his escape. Among others he makes them (the laws, or the state) say:—"Since you were begotten and nurtured and educated under us, dare you once to say you are not our offspring and servant, you and your fathers before you!" These are words which do not impress Japanese as anything extraordinary; for the same thing has long been on the lips of 'Bushido', with this modification, that *the laws and the state were represented with us by a personal being. Loyalty is an ethical outcome of this political theory.*

8. Character and Self-Control:

It was considered unmanly for a Samurai to betray his emotions on his face. "He shows no sign of joy or anger," was a phrase used in describing a strong character. The most natural affections were kept under control. A father could embrace his son only at the expense of his dignity; a husband would not kiss his wife,—no, not in the presence of other people, whatever he might do in private! There may be some truth in the remark of a witty youth when he said, "American husbands kiss their wives in public and beat them in private; Japanese husbands beat theirs in public and kiss them in private.

"Bushido teaches that men should behave according to an absolute moral standard, one that transcends logic. What's right is right, and what's wrong is wrong. The difference between good and bad and between right and wrong are givens, not arguments subject to discussion or justification, and a man should know the difference. Finally, it is a man's obligation to teach his children moral standards through the model of his own behavior: The first objective of Samurai education was to build up Character.

The subtler faculties of prudence, intelligence, and dialectics were less important. Intellectual superiority was esteemed, but a Samurai was essentially a man of action.

Discipline in self-control can easily go too far. It can well repress the genial current of the soul. It can force pliant natures into distortions and monstrosities. It can beget bigotry, breed hypocrisy or hebetate affections.

Be a virtue never so noble, it has its counterpart and counterfeit. We must recognize in each virtue its own positive excellence and follow its positive ideal, and the ideal of self-restraint is to keep our mind level—as our expression is—or, to borrow a Greek term, attain the state of 'euthymic', which 'Democritus' called *'the highest good'*.

No historian would argue that 'Toyotomi Hideyoshi' (Imperial Regent of Japan 1585–1591, regarded as Japan's second 'great unifier') personified the Eight Virtues of Bushido throughout his life. Like many great men, deep faults paralleled his towering gifts. Yet by choosing compassion over confrontation, and benevolence over belligerence, he demonstrated ageless qualities of manliness. [55]

In the history of Japan, 'Toyotomi Hideyoshi', is noted for a number of cultural legacies, including the restriction that only members of the Samurai class could bear arms and that all peasants be disarmed completely.

Toyotomi Hideyoshi

He financed the construction, restoration and rebuilding of many temples standing today in Kyoto. Hideyoshi played an important role in the history of Christianity in Japan, when he ordered the execution by crucifixion of twenty-six Christians, making example for those who wanted to convert to Christianity.

But apart from that, he ordered comprehensive surveys and a complete census of Japan. Once this was done and all citizens were registered, he required all Japanese to stay in their respective Han (fiefs) unless they obtained official permission to go elsewhere.

This ensured order in a period when bandits still roamed the countryside and peace was still new. The land surveys formed the basis for systematic taxation.

In 1590, Hideyoshi completed construction of the Osaka Castle, the largest and most formidable in all Japan, to guard the Western approaches to Kyoto. In that same year, Hideyoshi banned slavery or unfree labor.

Certainly as 'Nitobe Inazo' pointed out, we can read and recognize the elements of 'Bushido' in Hideyoshi's conducts, and of course there are similar accounts elsewhere too. For example:

Over 70 years before 'The First Geneva Convention', 'Matsudaira Katanobu 松平容頌' (1750–1805), the Lord of Aizu Domain (modern day of Fukushima Prefecture), produced two sets of formal rules for his Samurai army in 1790s, which codified the rules for '**Shocho Kinrei** 将長禁令' (Commanders) and the rules for '**Shisotsu Kinrei** 士卒禁令' (Soldiers).

These rules laid down the foundation code of conduct for modern standard military operations. *These rules codified 'the human rights' and 'protection of enemy noncombatants'*:

敵地といえども猥りに田畑を踏荒らすべからざる事。

"Regardless of whether it belongs to the enemy, trampling and ruining rice fields is forbidden."

敵地に入って、婦女を犯し、老幼を害し、墳墓を荒らし、民家を焼き、猥りに畜類を殺し、米金を掠取り、故なく林木を伐り、作毛を刈取べからざる事。

"In enemy territory, it is forbidden to rape women, harm the elderly and children, desecrate graves, torch the homes of commoners, slaughter livestock needlessly, pillage money and rice, cut trees without reason, and steal crops in the field."

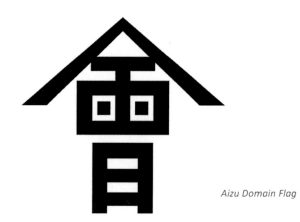

Aizu Domain Flag

Now, as 'Nitobe' explained in his book, 'Bushido' is the fountain of Japanese moral obligations, here the question might be: "then where is the root of 'Bushido' itself?" To answer that, here is what 'Mosi Dorbayani' has to say: *"Well, while some try to link it to Zen, Shintoism, Taoism or Buddhism, it is quite clear that 'Bushido', especially its codes of <u>'moral and ethics'</u> has nothing to do with any forms of religion, and although the teachings of 'Confucius' may have influenced 'the way of warriors' of Japan, in my view:*
'The source of 'Bushido' is the "Heart" of the warrior'.

I may as well add that, 'the way of warrior' in today's term can be:
'While treasuring life and respecting human values, seeing things through, assuring matters are resolved, and getting the job done' "

ACKNOWLEDGMENT: ABOUT THE CONTRIBUTORS:

Tetsuhiro Hokama, PhD - Hanshi, 10th Dan – Okinawa Kobudo & Karate

Tetsuhiro Hokama, was born in Taiwan in 1944 of Okinawan parents. Hokama, Hanshi began Karate as a child in 1952. His grandfather Seiken Tokuyama taught him the fundamentals of Shuri-te Karate. In 1961 his formal training began at the Naha Commercial High School Karate club. That same year he began training with the legendary Seiko Higa (1898 -1966) a student of Kanryo Higaonna (1853-1915) and Chojun Miyagi (1888-1953). It was at Higa's Dojo where he met Shinpo Matayoshi (1922-1997 Kobudo Master) and began learning Kobudo, Hakutsuru ken (White Crane fist) and Kingai-Ryu (a martial art that his father, Shinko Matayoshi 1888- 1947 learned in Manchuria).

Upon the death of Seiko Higa in 1966 Hanshi Hokama continues his training with one of Higa's top student Seiko Fukuchi (1919-1975) who was Seiko Higa's assistant instructor.

His Goju-Ryu karate is of a quality that can amaze even the most experienced karate practitioners. His speed and power is inspiring and his knowledge of vital points is vast. He is a researcher of the history of the indigenous Okinawa art of self-preservation known today as Karate and Kobudo. Tetsuhiro Hokama is truly a master of the "Old Ways".

Among many of his milestones:
- 1987 – Founded the Okinawa Prefecture Karate and Kobudo museum.
- 1989 – Chairman of the Okinawa Karate Gojuryu-kai.
- 1990 – Conducted a study of Chinese Kenpo (Shokakuken) in Taiwan.
- 1990 - President of Nishihara Machi cultural Association.
- 1991 – Appointed researcher for Kobudo by the Okinawan Government.
- 1992 – Published a calligraphy book on Okinawan proverbs. Awarded a testimonial by the Okinawa Karate Association.
- 1993 – Recipient of The Congress of The United States of America Services Award for Karate and Kobudo instructions.

He is a well-published martial scholar, among his publications in 2014 we can name: 'Timeline and 100 Masters' and 'The Seven Samurai of Okinawa Karate'. Hokama is a regular visitor of Noble facilities in Stockholm, Sweden with the aim to propose 'Karate Noble Prize', a managing institution based in Ryukyu Island.

He holds a PhD in Physical Education and recently appeared in the Learning Channel documentary "Top Ten Martial Arts". He has been featured in many foreign magazines – proof of his high international reputation.

http://www.tetsuhirohokama.net

Chris Gleen, is a Japanese Historian, Author, Radio - TV Presenter, Producer, Narrator, MC, Columnist, Helicopter Pilot and Martial Artist. Often mistaken for being British, he was born in Adelaide, South Australia in February 1968.

In 1985, Chris was selected as a Rotary Exchange Student, spending a year in Sapporo, north Japan. On his return to Australia, he attended the South Australian School of Broadcasting, commencing his radio career with 5MU, before being headhunted to capital city Adelaide stations 5DN, 102FM, and X-FM. Returning to Japan in 1992, he was employed by Tokyo station KTYO, and from its inception in 1993, Nagoya radio stations ZIP-FM and 79.5FM Radio-i. He currently hosts one of the top three rated radio shows in Central Japan.

Apart from his regular radio work, Chris Glenn is often seen on Japanese TV, in commercials and as a presenter for various programs. He is regularly called on as a presentation and motivational speaker, and as a consultant for international PR and marketing projects.

From April 1994 he was apprenticed to Ogawa Nobuo, one of just ten remaining samurai armor craftsmen remaining in Japan, learning samurai armor history and crafting.

Chris holds *Shodan* (black belt) in the sword discipline of *'Kendo'*, is ranked *Nidan,* (2nd degree black belt) in *'Chanbara'* sword-fighting, and is a student of the *'Shinpukan Dojo'*, studying *'Enmei Ryu'* and *'Owari Yagyu Shinkage Ryu'* styles of swordsmanship.

Chris Gleen, on the left holding Bokken

He is the author of English language book, 'The Battle of Sekigahara, the Greatest of all Samurai Battles' (http://booklocker.com/books/7721.html Booklocker, 2014) and the Japanese language book on samurai castles, 豪州人歴史愛好家、名城行く (Published 2015, Takarashima-Sha, Tokyo (http://www.amazon.co.jp/豪州人歴史愛好家、名城を行く-クリス・グレン/dp/4800237025). He writes a weekly column in Japanese for the worlds' most circulated newspaper, the Yomiuri Newspaper, and weekly columns on samurai history and culture for Japanese history magazine, *Rekishijin*. Chris contributes articles on Japanese history for a variety of magazines, web sites and periodicals. He is the founder and editor of bilingual web magazine, Japan World, (http://japanworld.info/) dedicated to promoting and preserving Japans' long history, deep culture, traditions, arts and crafts. He is currently preparing to write his doctorate thesis on samurai history and culture.

In 2005 he flew a light helicopter over 12,000km from Melbourne, Australia to Nagoya Japan in the self-produced Friendship Flight 2005 project. In 2006 he produced the Samurai Festival, bringing a samurai team to Australia where the first performance of the *Shutsujinshiki*, (the samurai pre-war ceremony) ever seen outside of Japan was shown. Similar events were staged in Los Angeles in 2009, and again in Sydney and Melbourne Australia in 2010, and became the basis for the annual Japan Expo in France.

Other positions held include.

- Member of the Japan Armor and Weapons Research and Preservation Society.
- Director of the Tokai (Central Japan) branch of the Japan Armor and Weapons Research and Preservation Society.
- Director of the Tokai Armored Samurai Warrior Team.
- Director of the Nagoya *Shinsengumi Dousoukai* Preservation Society.
- Captain of the Aichi Prefecture Warring States Samurai Team.
- Sword instructor to the Okazaki Castle Warrior Performance Team.
- Chairman of the Australia New Zealand Chamber of Commerce, Central Japan Chapter
- Media Director for the NPO, Helicopter Collective of Japan. (HCJ)
- Director of the Aichi Guide Network
- Sekigahara Tourism Ambassador

Further details can be obtained from Chris Glenn's management office, PPF (Past Present Future).

http://www.ppfppf.com

Contact office@ppfppf.com

ABOUT THE AUTHOR

Mosi Dorbayani, MSc, PhD, is an Executive Advisor, Educator and Consultant in international management and strategic leadership. He is Author of several professional books and a well-published Lyricist.

He is also the Co-founder and President of WAALM, an international awarding body in arts and cross-cultures based in the UK and Canada. As a Goodwill Ambassador, he serves several UN affiliated organizations and promotes cultural diplomacy.

He is a member of Academic Council on The United Nations System and is the recipient of 2010 *Human Rights Hero Awards*, conferred at the United Nations, Geneva.

He started martial arts by learning 'Gong Fu 功夫-中國武術' in 1976 and 'Karate 空手' in 1977 in style of 'Kanzen-ryu (a Shorinji-ryu branch 少林寺流拳行館唐手)', and attained his black belt in 1983.

Three years after achieving his 2nd Dan, he moved to the style of 'Shito-ryu 糸東流' in 1988 and followed his practice first by joining Kenshikan Shito-ryu Kenpo Karate 字面意思就是空手 (Kusano ha Shito-ryu) and then Shitokai 糸東会 (Founded by: Manzo Iwata Sensei).

He continued his practice in Shito-ryu and received his 6th Dan and 'Renshi-Instructor' license from Shitokai Association and National Hungarian Karate Federation (a member of WKF - World Karate Federation) and received his 7th Dan and 'Shihan – Master Instructor' title from Shitokai and the International Society of Okinawan-Japanese Karate (accredited by the International Traditional Karate Federation - ITKF).

In addition to Karate, he also holds 6th Dan in 'Ryukyu Kobujutsu 琉球古武術' and is certified in several Koryu styles, including 'Aiki-Jujutsu 合気柔術' and 'Tai-Jutsu 体術'.

His passion for martial science and martial history of Koryu Bujutsu has led him to become an avid practitioner of Kenjutsu (Samurai Art of Swordsmanship) and to follow 'Tenshinsho-den Katori Shinto-ryu 天真正伝香取神道流'.

During his martial sport practices, he achieved over 120 medals at national and international competitions in both Kata and Kumite (Team and Individual), 86 of which were gold.

In 1995 he was the first ever Founder, Manager and Technical Director for professionally paid International British College Karate Team. In 1996 he became a certified WKF regulated Judge and Referee in Kata and Kumite and was invited to act as the head-referee to several European and Scandinavian Karate and Kobudo Championships in Sweden, Denmark, Austria and Hungary.

Dr. Dorbayani is a three-time Mayor's award recipient for best coach and instructor in Hungary, which marks his trainees' success in achieving many European and World Cup championships in Kata, Kumite and Okinawan Kobudo.

From 1996 to 2003 he was the Chief Instructor of Shitokai in Hungary - European Union. From 1998 to 2007 he also served as a member of 'Technical Committee for National Hungarian Karate Federation and 'Martial Arts Technical Collage'. From 1999 to 2001 he served as Technical Advisor to 'World Martial Arts and Martial Sport Confederation' of Denmark. He was also amongst the official delegates for Central Europe at the Karate for Olympics campaign and performed at World Budo Gala in Copenhagen. He also represented 'The British All Styles Karate Association' in Central Europe from 1996 to 2000 and conducted many technical exchange programmes across various styles in the region.

In 1997 he established his own association (Kyokai) and after years of research on Koryu Bujutsu, in January 2004 Dr. Dorbayani's request to establish his own system in Karate was granted and he named his style 'KOJIDO TODI[KARATE]-JUTSU 固持道唐手術- The Way of Persistence in Martial Arts with Empty Hand'[56], and formed 'The Academy of Scientific Martial Arts' as a division to Kojido association, inviting instructors to provide education on Science of Martial Anatomy, Martial Physiology, Martial Philosophy as well as Japanese-Okinawan Culture and Language.

Eventually, his association developed to 'Sogo Bujutsu 総合武術 - Integral Martial Arts' and it is now one of the comprehensive martial arts associations with active training halls and disciples in Europe and Asia.

As the Founder and Headmaster (Soke) of Kojido, Dr. Dorbayani continues in advancing his art in Bujutsu and Martial Strategies and is teaching his followers 'The Way of Persistence' at his 'comprehensive martial arts association 固持道総合武術協会'.

From this author in other subjects:

- Successful Leadership – ISBN: 963 204 821

- Successful Business Organisation – ISBN: 963 210 234 7

- Successful Management – ISBN: 963 210 233 9

- Concise Economics – ISBN: 963 212 093 0

- Concise Human Resources and Personnel – ISBN: 963 212 096 5

- Moderation Management Enlightened with Philosophy – ISBN: 963 210 699 7

Official Sites:

www.dorbayani.com

www.mosidorbayani.com

www.waalm.com

http://renmei.wix.com/kojido

INDEX

M

148

150

REFERENCES AND PHOTO SOURCES:

[1] Mary Beard, J.A. North, and S.R.F. Price, Religions of Rome: A History (Cambridge University Press, 1998), pp. 47–48.

[2] http://www.kobukaijujitsu.com/grapplingstyles.html

[3] Iwona Czerwinska Pawluk and Walery Zukow (2011). Humanities dimension of physiotherapy, rehabilitation, nursing and public health. p. 21

[4] Reid, Howard and Croucher, Michael. The Way of the Warrior-The Paradox of the Martial Arts" New York. Overlook Press: 1983.

[5] Alter, Joseph S. (August 1992b). The Wrestler's Body: Identity and Ideology in North India. Berkeley: University of California Press

[6] "Huangdi". Encyclopædia Britannica. Retrieved 24 July 2011.

[7] Sun Tzu Biography and Introduction: Sun Tzu The Art of War and Strategy Site by". Sonshi. Com. Retrieved 2010-11-07.

[8] Reid, Howard and Croucher, Michael. The Way of the Warrior-The Paradox of the Martial Arts" New York. Overlook Press: 1983.

[9] Japan's Kodansha: An Illustrated Encyclopedia (1993) and The Connoisseur's Book of Japan Swords (1995)

[10] Ni Maoshing, (1995) - The Yellow Emperor's Classic of Medicine, Shambhala Publications, Boston MA

[11] Rhttp://www.acmuller.net/con-dao/analects.html

[12] http://www.schumannresonator.com/ http://svs.gsfc.nasa.gov/cgi-bin/details.cgi?aid=10891

[13] Dr. Lucio Maurino http://luciomaurino.com/

[14] You can view and hear samples by visiting the following links on Youtube:
https://www.youtube.com/watch?v=iiiznDpoapQ
https://www.youtube.com/watch?v=TslD9hLY8fQ&spfreload=1

[15] http://www.katori-shinto-ryu.org/

[16] To hear sounds of Kiai, consult the following links on Youtube:
https://www.youtube.com/watch?v=NyIL2cP5I2g https://www.youtube.com/watch?v=ds4jXl3yHEk

[17] Here is an example where you can hear 'Eiii' and 'Yaaa' in a Samurai fighting Battlefield: At 0:44 in this video clip, the command or charge starts with 'Eiii' (performed by Tom Cruise in the epic movie The Last Samurai) with a quick response by the warriors with 'Yaaa' and the rest of the action: http://youtu.be/nRcFxGxNglA?t=41s

[18] https://www.facebook.com/TheBattleOfSekigahara

[19] http://www.nichiren-shu.org/newsletter/nichirenshu_news/nichirenshu141.pdf

[20] http://blog.toyota.co.uk/muda-muri-mura-toyota-production-system

[21] http://www.collinsdictionary.com/dictionary/english/darwin

[22] Larson, Edward J. (2004). Evolution: The Remarkable History of a Scientific Theory. Modern Library. ISBN 0-679-64288-9 & http://www.encyclopedia.com/topic/human_evolution.aspx

[23] Nucleus Medical Media - written Mary Beth Clough & Ron Collins

[24] National Geoghraphy TV http://natgeotv.com/me/fight-science

[25] http://www.ncbi.nlm.nih.gov/pmc/articles/PMC1571064/

[26] https://www.youtube.com/watch?v=IqIL_Wx4AnA

[27] "Five Whys Technique". adb.org. Asian Development Bank. February 2009. Retrieved 26 March 2012

[28] http://www.botanicalgarden.ubc.ca/nitobe/inazo-nitobe

[28] http://shinbukan-kd.sakura.ne.jp/

[28] https://universalnutrition.com/features/breathingheartrate.html

[28] Roberts, A. R. (2000) An overview of crisis theory and intervention model. In A.R. Roberts (Ed.) Crisis Intervention Handbook. New York: Oxford University Press

[28] http://www.theorganicprepper.ca/

[28] http://www.yorku.ca/eye/eyemove.htm & Dr. Peter Hallett's chapter entitled Eye Movements which is Chapter 10 in Handbook of Perception and Human Performance Volume 1

[30] http://www.petalumaeyecare.com/yoga-vision-exercises/

[35] Stanford Encyclopedia of Philosophy by Stanford University. The discovery of two *Laozi* silk manuscripts at Mawangdui, near Changsha, Hunan province in 1973 marks an important milestone in modern *Laozi* research. The manuscripts, identified simply as "A" (jia) and "B" (yi), were found in a tomb that was sealed in 168 BCE. The texts themselves can be dated earlier, the "A" manuscript being the older of the two, copied in all likelihood before 195 BCE.

[36] In a lecture at TED - https://www.ted.com

[37] Colin Brookes, Woodhouse Eaves, Leicestershire

[38] http://www.prevention.com/

[39] http://www.nytimes.com/2012/04/22/magazine/how-exercise-could-lead-to-a-better-brain.html?pagewanted=all

[40] Boundless. "Types of Synovial Joints." Boundless Biology. Boundless, 05 Jan. 2015. Retrieved 11 Mar. 2015 from https://www.boundless.com

[41] Boundless. "Types of Synovial Joints." Boundless Biology. from https://www.boundless.com

[42] Tim Taylor, Anatomy and Physiology Instructor http://boneandspine.com/

[43] Cannon, Walter B. (1932). *The wisdom of the body*, 2nd Edition, 1939, Norton Pubs, New York

[44] http://thebrain.mcgill.ca/

[45] Krakauer, J.W., & Shadmehr, R. (2006). Consolidation of motor memory. Trends in Neurosciences, 29: 58-64.

[46] http://www.imdb.com/title/tt2103264/

[47] The Art of War, By Sun Tzu - translated by James Clavell - Random House Publishing 1983

[48] IRKRS - http://irkrs.blogspot.ca/2014/08/karate-do-kurofune-black-ship-of-karate.html?view=flipcard

[49] Armstrong, Hunter B. (1995) The Koryu Bujutsu Experience in Koryu Bujutsu - Classical Warrior Traditions of Japan. Page 19-20. ISBN 1-890536-04-0

[50] Knutsen, Roald (2004) Rediscovering Budo. Kent: Global Oriental. Page 22-23. ISBN 1-901903-61-3

[51] http://www.ryukyukobujutsuhozonshinkokai.org

[52] Imperial Household Agency (Kunaichō): 文武天皇 (42); retrieved 2013-8-22.

[53] In Feudal and Modern Japan Vol.1 (1896), Arthur May Knapp
http://ia700401.us.archive.org/11/items/feudalmodernjapa01knapuoft/feudalmodernjapa01knapuoft_djvu.txt

[54] Knapp, Feudal and Modern Japan, Vol. I, Ch. IV. Ransome, Japan in Transition, Ch. VIII.

[55] Brett & Kate McKay http://www.artofmanliness.com

[52] http://renmei.wix.com/kojido

PHOTO RESOURCES:

Front cover: Hands and Katana of the author - Photo by Marjan A. Dorbayani

P5: Photo of Mars - Archive of the author
Egyptian Mural - Public Domain

P6: India, Uttar Pradesh - Public Domain
Yellow Emperor - Creative Common - Public Domain

P7: "Shūkongōjin: clay sculpture". Photograph. Encyclopædia Britannica Online. Web. 17 May. 2015.
http://www.britannica.com/EBchecked/topic/301018/Japanese-art/images-videos/2860/shukongojin-clay-sculpture

P8 & P9: Ishiguro Ryu Jujutsu & Nawajutsu
Photo by: Broderick Jiff - Quirky Japan Blog
Samurai Training 1700 - Public Domain

P11: Kyoso Shigetoshi - Photo by Jay Holdings - Public Demo

P12 – 16: All images Creative Common Royalty Free
Arcenio J. Advincula, Publc Domain by Arcenio J. Advincula

P17 : Bubishi, Public Domain

P18 : Haticza Bernadett, Archive of Kojido Association

P19 : Both Images from the Archive of the author

P20 : Pinterest & Getty images Creative Common

P22 : Katori Shrine - Public Domain

P23: Wiki How

P25: Created and merged by the author

P26: Photo by Junji Kurokawa/Associated Press

P27: Wpid - Wallpapers

P29: Archive of the author

P31: Public Demo, Tokyo - Archive of the author

P32: Asai - shotokanciudadreal.blogspot.com

P32 & 33 Samurai on the horse - Created by the author

P34 Martial Buddha - Pinterest Public Domain

P35: Female Kata by Getty; the author doing Kata by Marjan. A. Dorbayani

P37: Merged and created by the author

P38 - 44 Public Domain, creative common

P44: The author doing Kata Photo by Marjan. A. Dorbayani

P45 & 46 :Paleoanthropology - The-Neanderthal Encampment, by Zdenek Burian

P46: The author showing Okinawan weaponry - Photo by Marjan A. Dorbayani

P50: Kumamoto Castle, Public domain, Creative common

P51: Yoshitora attacking a castle - Source Jmledwellwrite. word press.com

P52: Siege of ulsan battles fought between the mingkorea alliance and Japanese forces http://history.cultural-china.com

P53: Archive of the author

P54 - 55: Creative common

P57 & 58: Archive of Kojido Association

P60: Merged and created by the author

P61: ryukyu-bugi.com

P62-70: Creative Common, Royalty Free / Getty and Pinterest

P72 Archive of the author

Made in the USA
Middletown, DE
09 January 2021